# WALKS IN THE JULIAN ALPS

*Savica Falls  -  (Bohinj walk 2)*

# WALKS IN THE JULIAN ALPS

by

SIMON BROWN

CICERONE PRESS
MILNTHORPE, CUMBRIA

## ACKNOWLEDGEMENTS

Sincere thanks are extended to the Slovenian National
Tourist Board and all who have, in any way,
contributed to the compilation of this guide.

## DEDICATION

*To my son, Aaron Brown*

---

### Advice to Readers

Readers are advised that whilst every effort is taken by the author
to ensure the accuracy of this guidebook, changes can occur
which may affect the contents. It is advisable to check locally on
transport, accommodation, shops etc but even rights-of-way can
be altered and, more especially overseas, paths can be eradicated
by landslip, forest fires or changes of ownership.

The publisher would welcome notes of any such changes

---

*Front Cover:* Descending Prisojnik. Photo: G.Sellers

# CONTENTS

# INTRODUCTION

The Julian Alps (Julijske Alpe) are considered by many to be one of the finest examples of alpine limestone scenery in Europe. Although of relatively modest altitude, the peaks possess a formidable sense of grandeur and the terrain has a variety and diversity that is quite unique. The abrupt high mountain scenery of snow-capped peaks and barren ridges complement the pastoral broad-leaved forests that fringe lush lowland pastures. The relentless action of water on the porous limestone rock has resulted in a landscape endowed with a breathtaking display of natural features including enchanting lakes, deep cut gorges, crystal mountain streams and thundering water cascades. But perhaps its most appealing quality is the fact that the landscape has still been largely untamed by the hand of man and remains one of the last unspoilt regions of true natural mountain wilderness. Above all it is this wealth of untainted beauty that makes the Julian Alps one of the most satisfying walking areas in Europe.

The Julian Alps are the most easterly of the southern limestone alps and are situated to the south of the Karavanken, which are themselves part of the main European chain that forms Austria's southern border with Slovenia. The loftiest section of the Julians is concentrated in the north western region of Gorenjska. A section of the range overspills the frontier into Italy in the west but it will be the Slovenian Julians, with their unique charm, that this guide is concerned.

The individuality of the region is enhanced by the Slovenes, a friendly, hospitable people who share a strong national pride in the country's mountains and countryside. Evidence of this feeling is nowhere more prevalent than in the heart of the Julian Alps. A succession of agreements from 1924 secured environmental protection of the area and led to the present day boundaries of the country's largest national park being established in 1981. The park covers over 84,000 hectares and holds a rich variety of mountain flora and fauna, including many unique species. The park bears the name of Mt Triglav, the 2,864m peak that forms the centrepiece to the area, the highest summit in the Julian Alps and the highest mountain in Slovenia.

Mountaineering has long been a passion of the Slovene people and it was four local men from Bohinj that were first to reach the summit of Triglav in 1778. The Slovene Alpine Club (Planinska Zveza Slovenije) was founded in 1893 and began erecting a series of mountain huts to service the local peaks. The splendour of the Julian Alps was well known at the end of the eighteenth century amongst the nobility of Europe who, drawn by its enchantment, constituted the first tourists to the area. Eminent botanists of the same period also came to study the unique flora spawned by the combination of climatic influences from the Mediterranean and the northern Alps.

The Slovene people have always been passionately opposed to the commercial development of the alps, resisting several proposed projects, including the building of a cable car to the summit of Triglav. Tourism has developed, however, to become the region's largest source of revenue, but it is thanks to the determination of the Slovenes that visitors today can enjoy the same unspoilt beauty that attracted the first admirers to the area over 200 years ago.

The pasture lands in the valleys are still traditionally farmed with livestock. The lifestyle is a hard one with snow covering the ground for several months of the year, but despite this - or perhaps because of it - the people have a carefree contentment that is rarely seen amongst the affluent greed of city life. For the visitor it provides an unique insight into a forgotten lifestyle that harmonizes with the beauty of the mountains and the solitude of the countryside. You are invited, through this guide, to walk the valleys, the hills, the pastureland and forests. Explore the hidden secrets and, as with the Slovene people, the Julian Alps will find a resting place in your heart forever.

The Slovene people are mountaineers and mountain lovers and as a consequence the region is well mapped and criss-crossed with a network of marked mountain trails. Two long distance European paths cross the area: Route E7 runs from the Atlantic to the Black Sea and Route E6 from the Baltic coast in Denmark to the Adriatic. There are two high level traverses of the Julians to supplement the many routes that visit the area's mountain peaks. The paths have been generally designed to suit mountain traverses, a particular passion of the Slovenes, which invariably involve multi-day excursions with overnight stops in the many mountain huts. This is not to say that the area has little to offer the day walker - far from it. The peaks and valleys around the massif have their own individual charm which is scenically enhanced by the presence of the central high peaks. These areas too are well catered for by the many marked paths designed to guide the visitor directly to areas of special interest.

The object of this guide is to introduce walkers of all abilities to the splendours of the Julian Alps through a series of thirty walks. The walks have been especially chosen as an introduction to the area and vary considerably in character to take in the diversity of the landscape and the wealth of cultural and historic monuments. Paths explore the extensive broadleafed forests, visiting beautiful meadows of wild flowers, romantic clearings, canyons, sparkling streams and emerald green lakes that litter the dramatic mountain scenery.

The area has been covered using four regional centres as valley bases where the walks start and finish. These are Bled to the east of the range, Bohinj to the south, Kranjska Gora to the north and Bovec to the west. A description of each centre, along with details of available facilities, has been given at the beginning of the relevant section. Wherever possible the walks described are circular to make the most of each day trip. Where this has not been possible the appropriate details of public transport have been given to allow return to base the same day. Mention has also been made of any variations which can be taken in order either to lengthen or shorten the route described. The walks have also been chosen in such a way as to give the option of combining routes, allowing greater scope in planning an itinerary more suited to individual requirements.

## WAYMARKING

The waymarking of routes and maintenance of paths within the national park boundaries is of a high standard. Waymarks appear in the form of a "target" (a red circle around a white centre) painted regularly on trees and rock and are supplemented by red dashes. Signposts appear at major junctions giving details of the various route destinations and times. Waymarking outside the park boundary is a little more erratic. Each of the four centres has a network of numbered local paths which are waymarked with a varying degree of efficiency and where walks described in this guide coincide partly or wholly with sections of these routes reference has been made to the local route number.

## THE WALKS

Each walk begins with a brief outline of the route together with a list of suggested maps.

**Grading:** A scale of four subjective grades has been chosen to represent the difficulty of each walk, ranging from "Easy" through "Moderate" and "Difficult" to "Very Difficult". In addition to this a brief description outlines the nature of any difficulty encountered - ie. degree of exposure, routefinding problems etc. together with cautionary notes on special equipment requirements or dangers.

**Highest Altitude:** Gives the highest altitude reached on the walk.

**Lowest Altitude:** The lowest altitude reached on the walk. It should be noted that the difference between the two altitudes is not necessarily equal to the total ascent over the course of the walk. Many routes follow undulating courses that results in a much larger total height gain.

The **Walking Time** is the estimated time to complete the described route walking at a steady pace and does not include stops of any kind.

The general character of the walk is then briefly summarised describing any points of interest along the route. This is followed by a more detailed route description giving details of waymarking, possible variations and any public transport requirements.

Directions right and left are given in the direction of travel. Where this may lead to confusion, qualification has been made by use of the standard compass points - N, S, NW, NE etc. River banks are described in relation to the direction of flow or looking down the valley.

These walks have been chosen to provide an introduction to the walking potential that this corner of the Alps provides. I have had much enjoyment from them and it is my hope that you will too. It is also hoped that, through this guide, many of you may be inspired to return to the region in future years.

# HOW TO GET THERE

AIR TRAVEL

Arguably the cheapest and undoubtably the quickest way of reaching the Julian Alps is by air. The area is served by the international airport at Brnik, 35km north of the Slovenian capital Ljubljana. Daily scheduled flights operate from London with regular services from Birmington, Glasgow and Manchester. Flights also operate to America, Canada and Australia with services to Los Angeles, New York, Toronto, Melbourne and Sydney. A large number of international airline companies also carry out regular flights into Slovenia from the UK, Australia and Canada.

The price of a fixed date return scheduled flight from London is about the same as the equivalent journey by rail and is a good deal easier. Low cost summer charter services are available during peak season (July/August) and flights are run daily from UK regional airports as well as London. An alternative to a direct flight would be to take advantage of the large numbers of low cost charter services into major Europe capitals during the summer peak season and continue the journey overland by rail (see section on travel by rail for details of main overland traffic). Flights to the cities in north-eastern Italy (Venice, Verona or Trieste) would allow travellers to save a bit of money by taking advantage of the unbelievably cheap Italian rail system that connects direct to Ljubljana.

Regular bus shuttles run to Ljubljana from the airport and local buses also operate services to the city and to Kranj, 7km north of the airport, from where regular bus services operate to the north and east of the Julian Alps. Taxi services are also available at the airport. From the city of Ljubljana a comprehensive network of buses or trains connects to all the main centres described in this guide.

Avis or Hertz operate car hire services at the airport and this facility can be booked direct before departure.

An alternative to going it alone is to sign up with one of the increasing number of package tour operators. Last minute bookings can produce some real bargains although you will be faced with the disadvantage of being tied to one resort for the duration of the stay.

Independent travellers are subject to a nominal departure tax that must be paid at the airport check-in desk prior to departure from the country. The tax is payable in local currency only. Transit passengers and children under two years old are exempt.

## BY RAIL

Slovenia is linked to all European countries by a comprehensive rail network. Express services run from the majority of west European cities to the Slovenian capital of Ljubljana and all offer couchette and sleeping cars as well as full dining facilities. Typical journey time from Paris to Ljubljana is around 18 hours. Rail travel across Europe is not cheap and very often more expensive than the equivalent journey by air. But it can be a more scenically rewarding way of travelling through Europe, particularly as part of an extended tour of the continent. Express Services to Ljubljana run from Paris, Munich, London, Venice, Struttgart, Dortmund, Graz, Berlin, Turin, Rome and Zurich, with summer season car-ferry trains operating weekly from Hamburg, Dusseldorf and Brussels. Up-to-date European timetables and prices can be obtained from;

Thomas Cook,
PO Box 36,
Peterborough PE3 6SB

or

The International Rail Centre,
PO Box 303,
Victoria Station,
London SW1V 1JY

Appointed travel agents in America, Canada and Australia are also supplied with current information and reservations and bookings can be made through them.

The European Inter-rail ticket, available from British Rail, entitles the holder to a month's unlimited travel on the European rail network and half price travel on British trains and Sealink ferries across the channel. The cost of the tickets is equivalent to a standard scheduled flight from London. Use of the ticket whilst in Slovenia, and particularly around the Julian Alps, will be very limited but it does offer a chance to visit the area as part of a more extended tour of Europe.

Ordinary returns are valid for up to two months and also allow stop-offs on the way. The price is similar to the Inter-Rail ticket. Children under the age of four who do not require a special seat travel free of charge and children under the age of 12 are entitled to 50% discount.

Bled has two stations, one at Bled Lesce on the Tarvisio-Ljubljana line, the other, Bled Jezero, is on the Munich-Trieste line which also passes through Bohinj Bistrica. The nearest stations to Kranska Gora and Bovec would be at Jesenice in the north and Nova Gorica to the south from where the journey would need to be completed by bus. Express train services will only stop at Ljubljana where there are good bus connections to all resort centres.

## BY ROAD

Europe is linked by a comprehensive network of motorways but whichever route is taken the journey is not likely to take less than 30 hours travelling time, so it is advisable to allow at least two days if travelling from the UK. Although petrol is becoming an increasingly expensive commodity, for a group of two or more people the trip can work out cheaper than air travel. If travelling from the UK, the cross channel ferry link from Felixstowe to Zebrugge gives convenient access to the Belgian motorway system into Luxembourg from where the German autoroutes offer the quickest and cheapest route across the continent to Munich and south via Austria. The Alps form a natural barrier along the northern border of Italy and Solvenia. Crossings can be made from Innsbruck in Austria via the Brenna pass (1,374m) into Italy or from Salzburg using either the Wurzenpass (1,073m) or Loiblpass (1,067m) into Slovenia. Both these passes are steep (19% and 24% respectively) and the situation will be greatly eased by the opening of the Karavanja tunnel which, at the time of writing, is still under construction. For those who have the extra time, travelling this route by road gives an opportunity to spend some time enjoying the spectacular scenery of southern Germany and Austria before crossing the alps into Slovenia.

An alternative route would be to use the French Autoroutes south to Lyon before crossing the alps using the Mont Blanc tunnel at Chamonix or the Great St Bernard Pass (2,473m) to the Aosta Valley. This route offers the advantage of some spectacular scenery around the Mont Blanc Massif but does incur the extra expense of the French toll routes and the cost of using the Mont Blanc tunnel (which is not cheap). Once in northern Italy a route can be followed via Milan, Verona and Trieste into Slovenia using the Tarvisio-Rateče crossing in the north which is convenient for Kranjska Gora or the Gorizia-Nova Gorica crossing to the south which is then linked by good roads to Bovec via Tolmin or to Ljubljana. Access to the Trenta/Soča Valleys from this direction can also be gained via the Predel pass (2,753m) into the Koritnica Valley above Bovec. All border crossings are open 24 hours a day with the high passes subject to the prevailing weather conditions. Information is available locally from the Avto Moto Zveza Information Centre by ringing 061/341-341.

Once in Slovenia driving gives the advantage of complete independence to explore the region. Motorways are as good as any in western Europe and in line with other continental countries are subject to tolls which must be paid for in local currency. In the northern massif main valley highways are well maintained but minor roads to villages and valley heads can be narrow and potholed with gradients of 1:4 not uncommon.

Full details of requirements for driving in the country can be obtained from the motoring organisations at home, but I have listed a few of the important points to note when travelling independently.

Three grades of petrol are available in the country: Premium (86 octane), Superior (98-100 octane), 95 octane leadfree and diesel, the cheapest fuel available. Petrol can be purchased in dinars or using petrol coupons (*bons*). These are valid at all petrol stations and can be obtained from tourist information offices and some hotels. The coupons are not available to Slovenian nationals and must be paid for in foreign currency. A 10% discount is given if the purchase is made at border crossings, or from tourist offices before departure. The coupons are not available at petrol stations. Unused coupons can be cashed at the border when leaving the country.

Documentation required by the Slovenian authorities is much the same as other European countries. This includes a vehicle registration document (which must be in the driver's name), international driving licence and an international green card motor insurance, available from motor insurance companies at home. Foreign vehicles should clearly indicate the country of registration as well as the licence plate. Each vehicle should carry a safety triangle and a spare set of bulbs, and seat belts are obligatory for drivers and front seat passengers. Children under 12 must sit in the back. The following speed limits should be adhered to: 120km/hr on motorways, 60km/hr in built up areas and 100km/hr on open roads. Fines for road traffic offences must be paid on the spot and are expensive. If you pass a breakdown or accident you are legally required to stop and offer assistance.

The Slovenian Automobile Association (Avto Moto Zveza) operates a national breakdown service available by dialling 987. The nearest centre to the Julian Alps is at Ljubljana and is available 24 hours a day. It is advisable to get an estimate before leaving a car for repair as it is often costly. Automobile associations and motoring clubs at home will be able to give information on vehicle cover in the event of accident or breakdown.

Car hire is readily available in Slovenia and although usually too costly for the independent traveller can be useful for larger groups. Rates are quoted in £ sterling and start from about £22 per day for a small hatchback. The price allows unlimited mileage and includes insurance. Drivers must be over 21 and able to produce a current valid driving license. Substantial savings can be made if a car is booked from home as part of a package deal.

# TERRAIN AND CLIMATE

The terrain found in Slovenia is as varied as it is beautiful. To the north of the massif one could be forgiven for thinking the scenery to be Swiss or Austrian with snow-capped peaks rising above densely wooded valleys. The intoxicating aroma of wild flowers growing in the open pastures mingling with the scent of fresh cut hay drying in the sun lends the southern half of the range a more Mediterranean feel. This is due, in part, to the climatic influence of the coastal regions but also to the inevitable cultural influence of neighbouring

Italy. The area in general displays all the features of a classic limestone range: the porous rock fashioned into an amazing variety of natural sculptures, caves and deep gorges by the cascades of crystal clear water descending from the high lakes and streams. The underlying bedrock is a constant feature of all the walking routes, giving rise to intricate paths that weave a course around outcrops and boulders. Some sections of the more difficult routes have even been cut directly into the cliffs giving some exciting, but well protected, traverses. The limestone peaks have a presence far exceeding their modest altitude, shaped by ice and water to form a unique environment for flora and fauna, that makes the Julian Alps so special.

Much of the valley floors and lower slopes are tree covered. The moist climate favours the growth of deciduous trees over evergreens and the forest walks are particularly fine, with paths punctuated by beautiful flower carpeted glades of pasture and meadow. The upper tree line is fringed by the hardy larch and dwarf pines before the vegetation finally relents to barren rock and scree above where only delicate wild flowers, blooming from tiny rock crevices, can survive the extreme climatic conditions.

The rivers and lakes of the region are linked by a complex network of subterranean caves, caverns and water courses which give rise to a wealth of natural features. The walker should, however, not be complacent. Features that may appear quite tame during periods of extended dry weather may change considerably in character over the spring thaw or after periods of heavy rain. Dry stream beds are transformed into torrential rivers and small springs into foaming cascades.

Slovenia has a central European temperate climate which simply means that the summers are hot and the winters are cold. The Julians are often described as being "on the sunny side of the Alps". Certainly the weather is more stable than a coastal range but, more realistically, the region is subject to the same unreliable fluctuations as with any mountain area. It is not uncommon for snow to fall above 1,700m at any time of the year and is therefore essential that adequate equipment is taken before embarking on any trek into the hills. Weather forecasts are available at the local tourist information centres and it would be wise to check before setting off. For those more meteorologically minded Bled has a weather station at the end of the Ljubljana cesta with chart recorders of pressure, temperature and humidity.

The most reliable months for walking are July, August and September with average midday temperatures reaching over 23°C. The majority of the winter snow has disappeared by this time with only patches remaining above 2,000m and the weather patterns is at its most stable. Thunderstorms can be a problem in the afternoons, triggered by the high midday temps during June/July and it would be wise to avoid routes that traverse exposed ridges in these conditions. Where a particular route is considered prone to this danger mention has been made in the detailed description.

July and August are also very busy and food and accommodation are subject to a high season surcharge. Much of the accommodation will be full and public transport will be crowded. This must be weighed against the fact that many extra services are provided during the high season with transport connections and cable car access at their most frequent.

The best months for walking, therefore, are probably June or September closely followed by May and October. October has the additional advantage of the first of the autumn colours, although the weather is a little more unpredictable and of course the days are considerably shorter. During May and June patches of snow will still remain above 1,600m but you may feel that this is more than compensated for by the yearly rebirth of springtime, igniting the pastures and meadows that are such a feature of the valley walks, with a carpet of colour.

Water is scarce in many of the upper valleys during the summer months, leaving the stream beds dry. However, springs are tapped in high locations to provide a water source but it is advisable for walkers to prepare for the day's trek with an independent supply.

# ACCOMMODATION

## GENERAL

Tourism has been carefully developed in Slovenia over recent years. As each resort has expanded to cater for the increasing numbers of visitors to the area, great care has been taken to harmonise new buildings with both the natural landscape and traditional architectural styles. Where possible existing buildings have been converted to avoid unnecessary growth. The result is that accommodation is plentiful and well equipped without being obtrusive. Hotels are comparable with anywhere in Europe and provide all the amenities expected by the modern traveller. This is particularly true of the mountain resorts of the Julian Alps.

The wide choice of available accommodation ranges from highly priced luxury hotels through to campsites and youth hostels. A large proportion of visitors are accommodated in private rooms which are run along the same lines as Bed & Breakfast (usually without the breakfast) or guest houses. Self-catering chalets and apartments are also becoming increasingly popular, providing accommodation for parties of up to eight people, and can often work out to be very reasonable.

All accommodation in Slovenia is registered and rates are set at the beginning of each year. Prices vary according to the type of accommodation required and are usually quoted in German Marks (DM). Hotels, private rooms, apartments and chalets are arranged by the local tourist information offices who have a list of availability and prices. Passport details and length of stay are recorded on a registration form (Potrdilo), which forms part of a generally unused scheme whereby police can check that visitors are not breaking the law by sleeping rough or using unlicensed accommodation. Although it is unlikely that you shall be asked to produce the forms it is probably wise to hang on to them - just in case. Wild camping or sleeping rough will earn a stiff on the spot fine if you're caught.

Payment is made directly to the information office and will include a tourist tax which varies from 10 to 30 dinars per night. In addition a minimal registration fee is added to the bill. Stays of less than four nights will add another 20% to the nightly rate.

Accommodation rates are higher during the peak season months of July/August. Rates are about 20% cheaper during June/September with a further 10% off during May/October.

Campsites, youth hostels and the higher category hotels will complete registration and take payment direct at the reception. The beauty, of course, of a package deal is that all this is taken care of for you.

## HOTELS

Hotels in Slovenia are classified into several categories, based on level of comfort, services and available facilities. Classifications are: L (de luxe), A, B, C and D with standards compatible with the standard European star ratings. The L (de luxe) is equivalent to a five star rating down to the D class which would be roughly the same as a one star. A good compromise would be the B rating which offers comfortable accommodation at a reasonable price. The vast majority of the hotels at the centres used in this guide are either category A or B.

Hotels set their prices independently at the beginning of each season and as a consequence will vary according to the hotel category, the popularity of the resort, position of the hotel, facilities, month of the year and number of nights required. Category A hotels range from 55 to 200DM per person per night in a double room with breakfast with category B hotels between 70 and 100DM for the same arrangement. Children under the age of 7 are entitled to 30% discount. Half board is about 20% extra and registration fee and tourist tax account for another 2DM per person per night (children between the ages of 7 and 14 are charged 1DM). These prices are based on stays of over 4 nights. The rate works out considerably more per night for stays of 4 nights or less due to the 20-30% surcharge made for short stays. Single rooms also appear to be unpopular and when they can be found cost as much as the double rooms, so even if you're travelling alone you will find it just as economical to splash out on a double. Off-season discounts vary but can be up to 20% in June/September and 30% in May/October. Each hotel has a price list displayed at reception and local tourist information offices have a full list of available accommodation, together with prices. Hotel accommodation can be scarce during high season, despite the higher prices, so it is always wise to book in advance through international airlines, reservation companies or travel agents.

## MOTELS

It may be of interest to the motorist travelling to Slovenia that an increasing number of motels are being built beside main roads. In addition to accommodation motorists can obtain petrol, and there are shopping facilities and vehicle repair services. The positions of these motels are marked on the tourist map of the country available by writing to the Slovenian National Tourist Office. The office can also supply a full list of available accommodation together with a current price list.

## APARTMENTS & CHALETS

Self-catering holidays in self contained furnished apartments and chalets have become more popular in recent years and can prove to be the best alternative for small groups. Apartments are available to accommodate up to 8 people and prices range from 47DM per night for a double to 130-160DM per night for apartments sleeping up to 8. Reductions of 15% are available out of the summer season peak. Tourist tax is charged at 1DM per person per night with 50% reduction for children between 7 and 14 years old. As with hotels it is wise to book in advance during high season (July/August).

## PRIVATE ROOMS

Accommodation in private rooms (*sobe*) is plentiful and for the independent traveller can offer better value for money than standard hotel accommodation. The majority of visitors to the Julian Alps chose to stay in this type of accommodation but despite this rooms can still usually be found even in high season. They are similar to Bed & Breakfast accommodation or Guest Houses. As with hotels the rooms are graded according to comfort and facilities, and are generally very good value. Class 1 rooms have private bath/shower and WC, class 2 have washbasin with hot and cold water and access to a shared bathroom and class 3 have no washing facilities in the room.

On average the cost of a private room (double class 2) is less than half that of an equivalent double in a B category hotel. Class 1 rooms cost between 15 and 20DM and class 3 about 10DM. A 20% surcharge is levied for short stays and an additional charge of 1DM per person per night covers tourist tax. Signs are often displayed outside houses offering rooms and it may be worth enquiring if you plan to stay less than 4 nights. Single rooms, again, seem to be out of favour and cost almost as much as a double. The price does not include meals which may or may not be provided at extra cost. Once again substantial reductions are available for stays either side of the high season months of July/August.

Local tourist information offices administer the bookings for private rooms and have full details of prices and availability.

## CAMPING

In Slovenia camping (*autocamp*) is only permitted on official sites. These however are widespread and provide a range of facilities including hot showers, fresh water, shop, cafe, restaurant, toilets and electricity. The sites are usually large, some up to 9,000 pitches but smaller sites do exist and all cater for motorcaravans through to backpackers. Camping is generally very good value and, once again, charges will vary according to facilities on offer, size and location of the site and method of camping. High season prices will range from 16DM per night at a large site by the lakeside at Bohinj to 3DM per night on a small site in Bovec. Tax is fairly standard at 1DM per person per night. Children between the ages of 7 and 14 are given 50% discount with under 7s incurring no charge. Prices are also reduced up to 20% for long stays which can be particularly beneficial for groups. Further discounts are given at some sites to holders of an International Camping Carnet which can be obtained at home from camping clubs or national motoring organisations. The above price examples are given for high season and may be reduced by up to 30% outside July/August.

Wild camping is strictly illegal and is ill advised unless you really have to, when it would be advisable to seek permission from a local farmer for an overnight stop in the pastures. Camping within the National Park is also discouraged and largely unnecessary with plentiful accommodation provided by the abundance of mountain huts. Forced bivouacs within the park are also technically forbidden although obviously overlooked in exceptional circumstances. It should be stressed that no walk described in this guide should subject anybody to benightment on the hills!

Pre-booking is usually unnecessary and a full list of available sites in the area giving details of facilities and prices is available from the local tourist information office. The National Tourist Office can also supply a list of all the official campsites in the Julian Alps.

Camping gaz cylinders are not available in the country and cannot be taken on planes.

## YOUTH HOSTELS

Youth hostels are only common in large cities, Bled and Bovec being the only centres in this guide that offer the facility. Curfews after 10.00pm are enforced and buildings carry a total smoking ban. A bed in the dormitory style accommodation is expensive (20DM per night) when compared to private rooms widely available elsewhere in the towns. Technically you will require a Youth Hostel Association membership card in order to use the hostels and preference will be given to card holders during peak season. YHA membership can be obtained by writing to;

Trevelyan House, 8 St Stephens Hill, St Albans, Herts AL1 2DY

Accommodation is plentiful in Ljubljana and full details can be obtained from the Youth Hostel Authority, Farijalni Savez Jugoslaije, Mose Pijade 12/1, 11000 Belgrade, or the Slovenian National Tourist Office.

## MOUNTAIN HUTS AND REFUGES

Mountain hut or refuge accommodation (*Planinska Koča*) is largely beyond the scope of this guide, the ascent of Triglav being the only walk to utilise the facility, however, I feel it is worth mentioning some details in case walkers would like to extend their mountain experience by spending a night in a refuge. There is also the possibility that injury or bad weather may force a party to seek refuge at a hut. Many of the walks described in this guide pass mountain huts and walkers may wish to take advantage of the facilities.

There are over 35 refuges situated within the boundaries of the National Park. The huts are spaced about 3 to 5 hours walking distance apart and provide both refreshment stops for the day walker and overnight accommodation for the backpacker, climber or mountaineer. Sleeping accommodation varies from self-contained double rooms to large dormitories. Capacity also varies from a few beds to just under 200, dependent on the size and location of the hut. Even if a hut is full, overnight accommodation will never be refused but if a stop is planned it is best to book first. A basic, but usually wholesome, meal can be provided together with drinks and snacks. Most of the easily accessible huts will also offer a selection of souvenirs, maps and postcards. Visitors are also permitted to eat food that they have brought themselves although few allow cooking. Hot water can be purchased for making tea.

Most huts are open from mid June to the last week in September but some in the more remote locations are only open during the summer peak (July/Aug). Details of hut openings can be obtained from the local tourist information office who can also make reservations for overnight stops.

# GETTING ABOUT - TRAVEL WITHIN SLOVENIA

Bus services within Slovenia are run by a series of independent companies who, as a result of the fierce competition, have developed an extremely efficient and reliable network covering the area. Alpetour, Integral and Avtobusno podjetje are the main companies in northern Slovenia and operate routes to all the main tourist centres mentioned in this guide with comprehensive links to other major towns and cities throughout the country. During the summer season many extra services cover popular routes and special tourist buses operate between main centres and local attractions. All bus transport in the area can be considered cheap by western European standards.

The main bus station in Ljubljana is situated on the northern end of the city 35km south of the international airport at Brnik. Buses run hourly to Kranj, Kranjska Gora and Bled, with 5 weekday connections to Bovec. Transport connections between the valley bases are also very good with 3 daily direct connections from Bled to Kranjska Gora or an hourly service changing at Lesce. Hourly services also link Bled to the Bohinj Valley. Four buses each day make the impressive journey over the pass at Vrišič (1,611m) connecting Kranjska Gora to the Bovec basin (July/August only). Bus stations at each centre clearly display the timetable with further information available at the local tourist information office. Fares are collected on the bus with a small additional charge made for luggage - this is often overlooked unless the bus is crowded. Tickets can be bought in advance at bus stations and tourist information offices but there appears to be no real advantage in this. Details are given in the individual walk descriptions of any buses used.

Train services are not as well developed as the buses although during high season are considerably less crowded and offer a way of viewing the scenic countryside. The main train station is opposite the bus station in Ljubljana which is convenient for connections. Local train services hold no real advantages and buses undoubtably offer the most convenient public transport system. However, Ljubljana is connected direct to Lesce, where buses run hourly from opposite the station to either Bled or Kranjska Gora, and to Jesenice where again a bus must be taken on to Kranjska Gora. Change at Jesenice for train connection to Bled Jezero, situated on the far side of Lake Bled, and the Bohinj Valley at the town of Bohinj Bistrica. Tickets should be bought at the station or in advance from tourist information offices.

Driving offers the advantage of independence and is likely to be the mode of transport chosen if your walking holiday in the Julian Alps is combined with visits to other parts of the country or other areas of Europe. Having independent transport will give greater flexibility to explore the various valley bases described in the guide. Car parking is provided at all the popular departure points for walking and each centre has petrol stations, and vehicle repair facilities. Main road connections between the centres are good but secondary roads are usually narrow, steep, and poorly maintained and become more so the deeper into the massif one travels. The exception to this is the crossing from Kranjska Gora to Bovec over Vrišič Pass (1,611m) where the road is surfaced and well maintained throughout.

Taxis are readily available and convenient but quite expensive. Hitch-hiking is only recommended on popular routes to hiking departure points where much of the traffic will consist of fellow walkers and climbers. Hitching on main roads is not advisable due to its low success rate.

Many of the centres chosen operate mechanical access into the hills in the form of chair lifts, cable cars and gondolas. This gives the advantage of easy access above the tree line and enables the walker to explore the rocky peaks and ridges of the massif. Operation is frequent during high season (July/August) but tails off drastically during the spring and autumn months with only weekend operation during June and September. Where such access has been used full details of operating times and cost has been given in the individual route descriptions.

# MONEY

The Slovenian currency is the DINAR, divided into 100 PARA. Due to its post war political alliance with Yugoslavia the Slovenian economy has suffered more than most from economic recession. A succession of currency devaluations were imposed in an effort to stabilise the effects of massive inflation. Exchange rates were finally fixed to the German Mark on 1 January 1990 prior to Slovenia declaring independence. This appears to have temporarily stabilised the currency although it is always wise to check with banks before leaving. The result of this has been to bring prices in line with other west European countries.

There is still a restriction of 1,200 dinar per person that can be carried in or out of the country and for some inexplicable reason it is illegal to export 50 and 200 dinar notes. However, travellers may bring unlimited amounts of foreign currency into Slovenia in the form of cash, cheques, travellers cheques, credit letters etc. without any requirement to declare it. Unspent dinars may be re-exchanged on production of a receipt from any official exchange office.

Currency may be exchanged at authorised banks and exchange offices in travel agencies, trains, hotels and post offices, and may be re-exported if unspent. Lists of the current rates of exchange are displayed in exchange offices and may vary daily so it is wise to change only small amounts. Currency dealings with anyone other than the official exchange offices is strictly illegal.

Banking hours are 0730 to 1800 Mondays to Fridays. With some branches open on Saturdays 0730 to 1200 for payments and withdrawals.

Foreign currency can be exchanged for either dinars or for dinar cheques. Since 1983 dinar cheques have been available to the traveller as an alternative means of payment and have some advantages over cash. Payment in many hotels and restaurants with the cheques can entitle the holder to 10% discounts on the bill. This is not exactly the case in practice as several establishments do not provide the facility but cheques are useful for paying large bills in hotels etc. Hotels and restaurants that do accept dinar cheques will display a sign to that effect. Unused dinar cheques may be re-exchanged for foreign currency on leaving the country.

American Express, Access/Mastercard, Visa and Diners Club credit cards are readily accepted for payment in hotels and major shops etc. and can also be used to draw cash from the larger banks and tourist offices.

The best way of carrying money is in travellers cheques which are widely accepted in all Slovenian banks, tourist offices, post offices and most major stores, although commission charges will vary. Eurocheques are also widely accepted with a limit of 2,500din/cheque.

Duty free shops can be found in all the centres and at the airport which offer tax exemption on goods over the value of 1,000 dinar. This can be quite substantial ranging from 10% off chocolate to 64% off spirits and liqueurs. Goods available include beer, wine, toys, textiles, perfumes, and jewellery.

# THE LAW FOR WALKERS

As I have mentioned before, Slovenes are proud of their mountains and rightly so. The National Park covers a wilderness area of undisturbed habitat for many species of flora and fauna that have long been driven out of other parts of the European Alps. The park has been established to protect this for enjoyment for all and deserves everybody's respect. Slovenia has not, as yet, suffered from the effects of large scale tourism that has destroyed many other wilderness areas of Europe. It is **everybody's** responsibility to ensure that this unique area is preserved.

Visitors are therefore asked to comply with the park's code of conduct - only common sense really - but if everybody had that there would be no need for rules to protect an ever dwindling countryside:

Keep on marked trails; Take adequate bad weather clothing; Don't pick plants or disturb birds and animals; Refrain from making excessive noise; Take litter away; Close gates behind you; Don't damage alpine cottages, signs, visitors' books or altitude stamps; Abide by the displayed warning signs; Prevent forest fires; Don't cause rockfalls; Greet other mountaineers; Respect nature and the cultural wealth of the park and countryside.

Park wardens operate within the park boundaries and are charged with considerable authority. Any violation of the park rules may result in either a ban from the area or possibly an on the spot fine. Park rangers have badges and identity cards which they are obliged to show.

# CLOTHING AND PERSONAL EQUIPMENT

It is my hope that your holiday is free from bad weather but any mountain area is notorious for making its own weather regardless of the time of year and anyone planning any walking in the hills should be prepared for the worst. Walks in this guide have been chosen as an introduction to the area and as such have been planned to return the walker to the starting point easily within the same day. The ascent of Triglav is the only exception to this. The walks all follow waymarked trails and each description includes notes on variations, possible bad weather escape routes, and general mention of any particular difficulties the walker is likely to encounter. Equipment required will largely depend on the type of walk chosen - ie. high mountain ridge or forested slopes in the valley, the prevailing conditions and the ability of the party.

It should be noted that routes above 1,600m in spring or early summer are likely to encounter sizeable snowfields, in which case consideration must be given to ice axe and crampons. Walkers who are unfamiliar with these conditions and are not practised in the use of this equipment should avoid attempting the route. Snow lying in the north face gullies can dramatically increase rock scrambling difficulties and consideration should be given to rope, harnesses, and a selection of slings and Karabiners if any of the high mountain scrambling routes are in anything other than perfect summer conditions. Exposed peaks or mountain ridges should be avoided if thunderstorms are forecast.

There are consequently no definitive equipment requirements but, as a guide, I have listed what I consider to be the basic necessities on any outing into the mountains in summer.

Comfortable light walking boots - the majority of walks described do not require heavy mountaineering boots but a boot that affords a degree of ankle support is advisable. Many of the walks follow loose, bouldery terrain which could easily twist or sprain an unsupported ankle. Loop stitched socks, light shirt, sunglasses, hat, track suit bottoms, a pair of light trousers or shorts, pile jacket or a sweater, waterproof/windproof cagoule (a breathable fabric is ideal - but expensive), drinks container (1 litre), food for the trip, map, compass, camera, suncream (high factor), whistle, guide book (hopefully this one), small first-aid kit and a small (20-30 litre) rucksack to put it all in. By the way, rucksacks are *not* waterproof, whatever the salesman told you, so it's advisable to put all the gear in a large polythene liner.

Another good idea is some form of waterproof bag for the map. They will only usually stand up to a few inspections in the rain before turning soggy and falling apart. Large map cases that hang around the neck are fine but awfully cumbersome, especially on a windy day. An altimeter which, although far from being essential, is a useful aid to navigation in situations where visibility is restricted in low cloud or along forest tracks. Forests themselves can be deceptively cool so don't forget to take an extra something warm to wear even on the hottest summer day.

# FOOD AND DRINK

Slovenia is heavily influenced by the neighbouring countries of Hungary, Austria and Italy in many cultural aspects of social life and food is no exception. A strong Austrian influence is noticeable with a wide choice of heavy main courses and Strudels. Pastas from Italy are evident along with kebabs and rice dishes from the Mediterranean and goulash from Hungary, all spiced to local taste. In addition to western European dishes, a wide variety of local specialities are also on offer with meals designed to satisfy the heartiest of appetites.

Street stalls are a common sight in the larger towns and cities and provide quick snacks, serving hot dogs (*hot dogs*), beefburgers (*pljeskavica*), and delicious Turkish pastries filled with minced meat, cheese or apple (*burek*). More common in the towns around the Julian Alps are *gostiona* or self service cafes, usually found adjacent to supermarkets. These provide a similar range of snacks as the kiosk in addition to omelettes (*omlet*) filled with cheese (*sir*) or ham (*prsut*), kebabs (*raznjici*), sandwiches and drinks all at reasonable prices. Tea (*čaj*) is served without milk and is very weak while coffee (*kava*) is very strong. If you prefer your coffee milder ask for a "long" coffee (*dugacak kava*) and it will be made with more water/milk. Asking for a large coffee (*velik kava*) will only result in a large quantity of very strong coffee. Simple two course meals are provided at express restaurants, grill bars, mountain huts and inns (*gostina*) and are only slightly more expensive than the snack bars but still pretty cheap.

The majority of restaurants rely on the tourist trade and will provide menus with meals translated into both English and German.

Starters include a selection of soups (*juha*) followed by a wholesome main course which usually involves some form of heavily spiced meat, eg. mixed grill (*mesano meso*), steak in pepper sauce (*mučkalice*), lamb or pork casserole with rice and tomatoes (*djuveč*). Main dishes are invariably served with a vinaigrette side salad and may also include chips. The Italian influence is very strong to the west of the region and pasta dishes (lasagne, spaghetti and cannelloni) are common in Kranjska Gora and Bovec. Pizza restaurants are becoming more popular throughout the region and may provide the only alternative for vegetarians, who are not well catered for. The food is generally very good value although there may be a tourist premium charged on fish and meat dishes. A better value meal is often found away from the obvious tourist restaurants.

Local specialities vary from valley to valley but ones to look out for are buckwheat porridge (*heljdini žganci*) with stew (*paprikas*) or goulash (*gulas*) and Vodnik pie (*vodnikova pogača*).

Cheese is still manufactured by traditional methods on the high pastures in summer. It is golden-yellow with an aromatic taste reminiscent of walnut and is marketed through small cooperatives and sold locally.

Ice-cream is popular in Slovenia and is available in a multitude of colours and flavours from the many ice cream parlours, which also tempt the unwary with a range of cream pastries and strudels.

Selections of many excellent locally produced wines are available and it is rare to encounter anything that is undrinkable. Popular wines from the regions of Primorska, Stajerska and Dolenjska include a range of Rizlings - *Jaski* a sweet wine and *renski* the dry version. Slovenes are also fond of spirits which are both incredibly cheap and very strong. Maraska market a fine selection of potent fruit brandies. Sljivovica is a clear brandy made from plums and *travarica*, a herb brandy, both of which are worth a try on your last night. The local beer (*pivo*) is cheaper and every bit as good as the more familiar imported brands.

Supermarkets are generally well stocked and offer a wealth of heavily smoked meat, sausages and salamis and a good selection of hard cheeses. Bread ranges from the heavy German *Schwarzebrot* - literally black bread - to white loaves, rolls and French sticks. The wholemeal revolution hasn't hit Slovenia yet and high fibre bread is impossible to come by. Rolls with a variety of meat and cheese fillings will be made up on request and provide a cheap snack to take along on the day's walk. Dried food is also difficult to find, with only the larger stores carrying a small selection of soups. A wider selection of fruit and vegetables can be found in greengrocers or on market stalls. Vegetables tend to be limited by the local culinary requirements with large stocks of onions, chillies and peppers but very little else.

# PREPARATION

It is fairly obvious to say that an enormous amount of time can be saved and difficulties avoided by thorough preparation before leaving. The majority of people planning a trip to the area only have a limited amount of time (holidays etc.) and therefore any preparations that can be made at home will effectively maximise the time available for walking.

## MAPS

The Slovenian Julians are covered by two 1:50,000 maps published in 1988 by Planinska Zveza Slovenije (PZS):

PZS 50m Julijske Alpe-Mountain map West part
PZS 50m Julijske Alpe-Mountain map East part

These maps give an overview of the area and cover all routes described in this guide. Major waymarked footpaths are highlighted and although not really detailed enough for ground work are excellent for planning a first trip to the region. A good alternative to these would be the single 1:50,000 PZS map entitled Trglavski Narodni Park (Triglav National Park). Again it is suitable for planning trips to all the centres in this guide. The map highlights major waymarked routes, and information about the park flora and fauna together with natural and cultural sites of interest are printed on the reverse in English.

Maps are considerably cheaper to purchase in Slovenia and are widely available from tourist information offices. Each centre produces 1:25,000 local walking maps with local waymarked routes highlighted together with information about the area printed on the reverse in English. All walks in this guide are accompanied by an individual route map but it is still advisable to carry an additional map of the area for a number of reasons. Should the route be lost for any reason it may be necessary to use a map as a navigation aid in order to rejoin the path. Reference may therefore be required to distant landmarks beyond the scope of individual route maps. A map will also be useful in allowing parties to plan variations on the suggested routes in this guide and it is always fun to identify distant peaks and features from viewpoints. It goes without saying that maps are of little use unless somebody in the party is familiar with their use.

## Bled

There are two maps of Bled and its environs, available locally;

Karta Sprehodov In Izletov Bled z Okolico (Bled & surroundings walking map) 1:25,000 published by Inštitut za Geodezijo in Fotogrametrijo.

Bled Načrt Mesta (Bled Town Map) 1:6,600 Published by Inštitut za Geodezijo in Fotogrametrijo.

## Bohinj

An excellent 1:20,000 map produced by PZS entitled Julijske Alpe-Bohinj covers the lake, the Vogel ski area to the south and extends to the lower part of the Triglav lakes valley to the north. All trails are highlighted and the detail makes it invaluable for walks in this area. Also available locally is an aerial photograph that has been highlighted with local footpaths. The plan has no scale but is useful for walks in the upper Bohinj Valley between Bohinjska Bistrica and the lake.

## Kranjska Gora

A local 1:25,000 map covers the Sava Dolinka Valley from the Italian border in the West to the village of Gozd-Martuljek and extends south to cover walks from Vršič. The map is published by Inštitut za Geodezijo in Fotogrametrijo and is available from local tourist information offices. In addition to highlighting local walks mountain routes are also marked. PZS also produces a very good 1:20,000 map

Lake Bled and castle (M & T Leafe)
The Black Lake  (M & T Leafe)

entitled Julijske-Triglav. This covers the area to the south east of Vršič around Triglav. It is useful for walks from Vršič and the upper Trenta Valley.

*Bovec*
As with Bled two maps have been produced by Institut za Geoezijo in Fotogrametrrijo to cover the Bovec basin: a 1:4,000 town plan (Bovec Načrt Mesta) and a 1:25,000 map showing all local walking routes entitled Turistična Karta Bovec z Okolico.

PZS maps should be available from large outdoor shops or from specialist map and book shops. If there is any difficulty in obtaining maps to the area write to:

Edward Stanford Ltd
12 Long Acre
London WC2

Further information may be obtained by writing to the Slovene Alpine Association in Ljubljana.

## INSURANCE

It is always a wise precaution to take out insurance for any holiday. In keeping to the marked trails there is little risk of an accident occurring but the possibility still exists. General holiday insurance is fine and policies can be supplied at comparatively low cost, but do make sure you are covered for hillwalking. If you find this is not the case it is worth investing in one of the many policies designed specifically for the walker. Such policies are usually arranged through clubs and other outdoor organisations and in addition to the normal holiday insurance have optional cover to include personal accident, loss or damage of equipment and expenses incurred during any accident or mountain rescue operation. If there is any difficulty finding a suitable company try the classified section of one of the popular climbing or hillwalking magazines.

## POLICE

The authorities maintain a high profile in the area and are usually

*The Vintcar Gorge . Photo: M. & T.Leafe*

armed, which initially may be a little intimidating. However they are invariably friendly and are anxious to help visitors to the area whenever possible. It is worth remembering though that the police do possess awesome powers so it is wise not to provoke them. Passports, accommodation certificates and visas may be inspected at any time and should always be carried. Police stations are signposted and the national emergency number is 92.

Signs showing a picture of a camera with a cross through it should be taken very seriously. It is illegal to photograph military or strategic installations. This includes railway stations and bridges etc. The area which this guide is concerned with, thankfully, has many photographic opportunities.

## VISAS AND RED TAPE

Holders of a full UK passport or one from any other EEC country will not require a visa for stays of up to three months - long enough for most holidays. Extensions are difficult to arrange and for longer stays it is often easier to leave the country and return for a fresh stamp.

Australian, Canadian and USA passport holders need a visa which is issued free. New Zealanders and holders of British Visitors' Passports will have to pay a small charge.

# HEALTH

The standard of health in Slovenia is generally very good. Mains water is chlorinated and therefore drinkable although to avoid the all too common upset stomach you may wish to begin by drinking bottled water, which is freely available. High mountain streams are usually a reliable source whereas the valley rivers are best avoided. On the whole it is safer to use purification tablets for any natural water source (Micopur are expensive but do not taint the water.)

Milk is pasteurized and local meat, poultry, seafood, fruit and vegetables are safe. It may also be an idea to bring along some indigestion tablets if you're not used to rich, spicy food.

One sure way to reduce the risk of any general health problems is to embark on some kind of fitness program before you leave. If you walk regularly in the hills the routes described in this guide should pose no problem. It is worth noting, however, that ascents and descents in the Julian Alps can be long and a greater initial level of fitness will inevitably lead to greater enjoyment of the trip. The best exercise for hillwalking is hillwalking but good substitutes are cycling, swimming or jogging. Don't forget the small everyday opportunities like walking to the shops instead of taking the car, or using the stairs instead of the lift.

## FIRST AID

A basic understanding of first aid is useful in everyday life but in the mountains, where help may be hours away, it can literally make the difference between life and death. This guide can only outline a few basic principles and it is suggested that individuals who are not familiar with first aid techniques seek additional information from one of the many books that cover the subject in greater depth.

It is always wise to carry a small first aid kit the contents of which will largely depend on the individual's knowledge but should contain at least: a couple of sterile bandages, one large triangular bandage, sticking plaster, safety pins and sterile gauze. Medication should include painkillers.

If involved in any accident, either your own or somebody else's, the first priority must be to your own safety. Approach the incident calmly and systematically check the condition of the casualty.

1.  CHECK BREATHING - Clear the airway by physically removing any visible obstructions and tilt the casualty's head back. Commence artificial resuscitation until the casualty starts breathing. In the absence of any pulse commence external cardiac massage until the heart starts to beat. On restoration of blood flow and breathing place casualty in the recovery position.

2.  CHECK FOR SEVERE BLEEDING - Apply direct pressure on the wound and elevate the limb.

3.  BROKEN BONES - Do not move casualty if any spinal injury is suspected. Immobilise broken limb in the position most comfortable for the casualty using improvised splints.

4.   MONITOR CONDITION - Keep casualty comfortable and warm. Reassure casualty until help arrives. Monitor condition.

The mountain rescue service - Gorska Resevalna Sluzba or GRS - consists of well trained teams of volunteers. The rescue work is carried out free of charge. Any accident must be reported to the nearest reporting post. These can be mountain huts, police stations, remote farm houses. All reporting posts have a sign with the letters GRS displayed. Help may also be summoned using the international distress signal. Use a whistle to give six regular blasts repeated at intervals of a minute. The reply is three signals per minute.

## MOUNTAIN HEALTH

One of the most common complaints that can ruin a walking holiday can be blisters and one of the most common causes is ill fitting boots. Boots should be worn in without being worn out. One pair of loop stitched socks should be worn and these should be changed regularly. If you feel any rubbing in the boot stop and attend to it. Quite often a patch of moleskin over the offending area will prevent any further deterioration (sticking plaster works just as well).

Hyporthermia is responsible for the deaths of many walkers. Even in the summer months attention must be paid to the weather and plans adjusted accordingly. Weather forecasts are broadcast daily in English on the radio during the summer. In addition tourist information offices can give an up-to-date forecast. Hypothermia occurs when the body loses heat faster than it can generate it. Walkers are at greatest risk wearing wet clothing in a cold wind. The symptoms are uncontrollable shivering followed by drowsiness, lethargy and an almost drunken like incoherence. The casualty should be warmed immediately by covering in extra clothing. This should be put on over existing clothing even if it is wet. Talk to the casualty continually and feed with warm drinks and sugary food. Medical help should be sought as soon as possible.

Altitude sickness does not have serious effects below about 2,500m. However it is not the height itself that is the problem but how quickly the height is gained. Walkers unused to altitudes may experience slight headaches accompanied by a rapid heartbeat. A short rest is usually sufficient to cure this but should the symptoms persist it would be wise to lose height and rest for a time at a lower altitude. Altitude sickness can affect anybody regardless of level of fitness.

Sunburn is very serious and a danger perhaps underrated by too many people. The strength of the sun increases with altitude and combined with wind and the reflection from surrounding rock, snow or water can burn sensitive skin in no time at all. Use a high factor suncream at all times paying particular attention to the ears, eyes, lips and nose. Wear a hat and sunglasses. If you do get burnt apply a total block cream until the skin has healed and cover the affected area as much as possible.

Snakes do exist in Slovenia, notably the adder and mountain viper, the latter being identified by its almost black colouring with characteristic zigzag markings. The saying that they're more afraid of you than you are of them still holds true and the chance of seeing one is slim. The noise of an approaching walker is usually sufficient to send any snake into hiding. Take sensible precautions and refrain from poking around under logs or boulders. If you should be unlucky enough to be bitten try to remember what the snake looks like and seek medical advice. Bites are rarely fatal, small children being at greatest risk.

A period of wet weather will encourage salamandas into the open. The region has two species the mountain salamanda (black) and the fire salamanda, recognisable by distinctive yellow markings on its black body. These look fearsome but are in fact harmless.

Rabies is endemic throughout the whole of mainland Europe. For those at high risk vaccination before arrival should be considered. If bitten by an animal it would be wise to seek medical attention immediately.

Basic precautions for mountain safety should be taken by all walkers before setting off for the day. Plan your route thoroughly with due regard the ability of the weakest member of the group. Don't overestimate the physical ability of the group. Give due regard to the weather forecast and don't hesitate to cut a section from your itinerary or turn back if the weather deteriorates. Water can be scarce in the hills during summer so it is important to take enough liquid for the day's trip. The thick canopy of beech trees that is such a feature of the valleys and lower slopes is very effective at obscuring the sun and even in the middle of summer forest routes can remain quite cool. Keep to the marked trails especially on the high mountain walks where the nature of the terrain and descending cloud can combine to make any route finding very problematical. Mountain paths that cross sections of easy angled rock are invariably littered with scree and other loose material, and special care should be taken to avoid dislodging any debris on other walkers. Leave notice at the hotel giving your intended route and expected time of return. Carry adequate equipment including enough spare clothing and food. Always carry map and compass and know how to use them.

The emphasis throughout this guide is on enjoyment and enjoyment of the hills involves being prepared, being wary, being sensible and being safe.

## MEDICAL CARE

While staying in Slovenia British citizens are entitled to free medical care and full use of the medical services of any hospital etc. on production of a valid passport, in agreement with the reciprocal rights signed between the two countries (a small nominal fee is charged to cover administration costs). Citizens of the USA, Canada, and Australia will be required to pay for any medical facilities used.

There is no requirement for vaccinations to visit Slovenia though, as with all countries, the situation may be subject to change at short notice. Doctors are provided with up-to-date requirements. It is wise to be up to date with tetanus and it may also be a good idea to see your doctor or dentist for a check up before leaving, particularly if you're planning a long stay, simply because it's much easier at home than abroad.

# SLOVENIA - THE PEOPLE AND CULTURE

The end of World War I in 1918 brought with it the downfall of the Austro-Hungarian Empire and the end of 400 years of domination by the Hapsburgs over this European territory. Unrest continued until, in a state of turmoil, the area was thrown into World War II. The borders of Yugoslavia were only ratified after the end of World War II in 1945. The republic emerged liberated and unified under the communist leader Tito.

Tito set about solving the diverse nationalist problems of the country by establishing independent rule within each of the six republics. He himself headed the central government which sat in the capital of Belgrade and was made up of representatives from each republic. Since Tito's death in 1980 the system he established had continued with each representative serving a one-year term as head of the government.

Slovenia was probably the most economically advanced of all the republics due in part to its beneficial geographical position to the neighbouring countries of Austria, Hungary, and Italy. The result is that Slovenia enjoyed the highest standard of living in Yugoslavia. The shops were well stocked, services reliable and efficient, and facilities provided to serve the growing number of tourists visiting the area each year were excellent.

The republic was ripe for independence and so it came as no surprise when Slovenia finally severed ties with the crumbling Yugoslavia.

The Slovenes first settled in the valleys around the Julian Alps after the collapse of the Roman empire in the fifth century, clearing pastureland for livestock and growing crops in the open valley plains. These traditional farming methods are still much in evidence today. High pastures are used to graze the livestock - cattle, sheep, and goats - in the summer months which releases the fertile lowlands for growing potato, maize and hay to sustain both man and beast through the cold winters. During the autumn months large stores of wood are still required to heat the homesteads.

The area had a succession of overlords which heavily influenced the cultural development of the Slovenes. Artistic development blossomed in the gothic period of the fifteenth century and flourished under baroque influences from the mid seventeenth to the late eighteenth century. Ljubljana, the political, commercial and cultural capital of Slovenia, has a fine architectural inheritance from this affluent period and one of the finest examples of the baroque golden altars can be seen in the church on the island at Bled.

Influences from the Mediterranean, alpine and pannonian cultures merge to make Slovenia one of the most interesting regions for visitors in Europe. Despite this, the Slovenes still maintain a strong sense of national independence and are rightly proud of the traditions and folklore that strengthen their own identity. This is most obviously seen through the widespread use of the Slovene language.

Relationship with the British is very good in Slovenia and contrary to popular myth English is fairly widely understood in hotels, tourist offices, restaurants and shops. German and Italian is also widely spoken in all areas and may help you out when all else seems lost. The Slovenes themselves are relaxed, friendly, hospitable and very helpful and even if your stay is short it would be polite to return the courtesy by at least familiarising yourself with some greetings.

The most common greeting, and one you'll hear echoed along the walking trails is *Dober dan* - Good day. Extensions of this are *Dobo jutro* - Good morning or *Dopoldan* - Morning! and *Dobro Vece* - Good evening. *Zdravo* is less formal and can be used for Hello or Goodbye. All greetings are much more effective if they are delivered with a smile. Below is a short selection of words and phrases that may be useful during your stay. This is by no means a comprehensive list and should you feel you may wish to explore the language further it would be useful to take along a phrase book or dictionary.

| | |
|---|---|
| please/thankyou | prosim/hvala |
| yes/no | da or ja/ne |
| toilet | toalet |
| men/women | moški/ženski |
| entrance/exit | ulaz/izlaz |
| push/pull | rici/vleci |
| | (saves embarrassment at shops, post offices and banks etc.) |

| | |
|---|---|
| police | milica |
| hospital | bolnica |
| bus station | autobusna postaja |
| rail station | zelezniska postaja |
| tourist information | turisticne informacije |
| | (tourist agencies offer similar |
| | services and may appear |
| | under company names, |
| | eg. Globtour, Kompass etc.) |
| post office | PTT posta |
| bank | banka |
| telephone | telefonska govorilnica |
| sun | sonce |
| wind | veter |
| rain | dež |
| cloud | oblak |
| storm | nevihta |
| fine weather | lepo vreme |
| bad weather | slabo vreme |
| help! | na pomoč! |
| bridge | most |
| hayrack | kozolec |
| barn constructed of several hayracks | topolar |
| source | izvir |
| mountain | gora |
| hut | koča |
| (mountain) hut | (planinska) koča |
| hostel | dom |
| summit | vrh |
| lake | jezero |
| pasture | planica |
| rock | skala |
| col | sedlo |
| waterfall | slap |

# FURTHER INFORMATION

## NATIONAL HOLIDAYS

January 1st, 2nd - New Years Day; May 1st, 2nd - Labour Day; July 4th - Veterans Day; November 29th, 30th - Republics Day.

Slovenia is largely Roman Catholic and in addition to the above the following religious dates are observed: April 27th, November 1st, December 25th. Slovenia also celebrates an Uprising Day on July 22nd. If any of the above dates fall on a Sunday (except Veterans Day) the following Monday becomes a national holiday too. On these days and on Sundays all shops are closed.

Many sporting and cultural events are held annually in the area. The European ski jumping final is held at Planica near Kranjska Gora on the last weekend in March and the May Day rowing regatta at Bled. The official opening of the summer season also takes place at Bled during mid June from when classical music concerts are held each Monday on the island. Also at the end of June is a regatta held on Lake Bohinj. Bled and Bohinj have an annual Peasant Wedding, a two-day event that takes place at the end of July. The ceremony is performed in traditional style and colour and includes many aspects of ancient folklore and customs. Traditional customs also accompany the bonfire night on Lake Bohinj in August and the September Cow Ball to celebrate the return of the cattle from the summer pastures to the valley. Dates may vary each year and a full calender of events can be obtained from the National Tourist Office.

## POST OFFICE

Main post offices are open 0800 to 1800 Monday to Friday and 0800 to 1200 on Saturday with occasional Sunday hours in larger cities. International phone calls can be made from any post office. Phones are located in numbered sound proof booths and a running meter advises of the cost. Payment is made at the counter. Phone boxes take 2, 5 and 10din coins which makes them impractical for international calls although card phones are becoming more popular and are more convenient for this purpose. There is no cheap rate. International country codes are;

Great Britain: 99 44
Irish Republic: 99 353
Australia: (only through operator) 901
United States and Canada: 99 1

Don't forget to omit the first digit of the local code when direct dialling.

Stamps are, of course, sold but are also available for postcards from souvenir shops.

## BANKS

Bank opening hours vary slightly from town to town but are generally from 0730 to 1800 Monday to Friday and 0730 to 1200 on Saturdays. Banks will change travellers cheques and Euro-cheques and also give cash withdrawls on major credit cards.

## MEDIA

Foreign newspapers are available in the four regional centres during peak season.
BBC world service: 13 - 49m short wave throughout the day.
Radio Ljubljana, Daily English broadcasts: Tourist news, weather and international news on 88.5, 96.5, 100.1 Mhz VHF.

## INFORMATION CENTRES

Tourist Information Centre, Titovall, 61000 Ljubljana.
      Tel: 224-222, 263-55
Triglav National Park, Kidriceva 2, Bled, YU-64260.
Automobile Association: Avto Moto Zveza Slovenije; Titova cesta
      138, 61000 Ljubljana. Tel: 342-661.
Slovene Alpine Association (PZS): Dvoržakova 9, Ljubljana.
JAT, Miklosičeva 34, Ljubljana.
KOMPAS, Miklosičeva 11, Ljubljana.

## NATIONAL TOURIST OFFICES

Great Britain: Slovenian Tourist Office: 143 Regent Street, London
      W1. Tel: 071-734-5243/8714.
USA and Canada: 630 Fifth Avenue, New York, NY 10020

## EMERGENCY SERVICES

A 24 hour Police, Fire and Medical service is available throughout Slovenia. The emergency numbers are
police - 92, fire - 93, hospital - 94.

## OTHER USEFUL NUMBERS

### Bled

Travel agencies and tourist information: Tourist Association Information: 77-838; Tourist Association Office: 77-409; Generalturist: 77-234; Globtour: 77-909; Kompas: 77-245; Alpetour: 77-575; Kvarner Express: 77-685; police station: 77-152; medical centre: 77-181; post office: 77-200; bank 77-171; bus station: 77-357; rail station - Jezero: 77-243; Lesc: 77-118; Taxi: 77-578.

### Bohinj

Travel agencies and tourist information: Tourist Bureau - Ribčev Laz: 76-370; Alpetour - Ribčev Laz: 76-441; Kompas - Ribčev Laz: 76-471; police station - Bohinj Bistrica: 76-117; medical centre - Bohinj Bistrica: 76-120; post office - Ribčev Laz: 76-460; Bank - Bohinj Bistrica: 76-221; rail station - Bohinj Bistrica: 76-122; taxi - Srednja vas: 76-153; Ribčev Laz: 76-413; Vogel cable-car: 76-301.

### Kranjska Gora

Travel agencies and tourist information: Tourist Office: 88-768; Kompas: 88-161; Integral: 88-413; police station: 88-522; medical centre: 88-426; post office: 88-491; bank: 88-430; taxi: 88-388, 88-198; ski lifts: 88-414.

### Bovec

Tourist agencies and information: Tourist Office - Avtopromet Gorica: 86-064, 86-123; Kompas: 86-101, 86-202; police station: 86-050; medical centre: 86-057; post office: 86-000; bank: 86-017; Kanin Gondola: 86-098.

## CONSULATES

British Embassy: Belgrade, Generalna Ždanova 46. Tel: 645-055
Australian Embassy: Belgrade, Čika Ljubina 13. Tel: 624-655

Canadian Embassy: Belgrade, Proleterskih Brigada 69. Tel: 434-524
American Embassy: Belgrade, Kneza Miloša 50. Tel: 645-655

## TIME

One hour ahead of GMT and BST.

# BLED

There are many attractive mountain resorts in Europe but perhaps none more so than the small town of Bled (501m). Situated on the fertile Gorenjsko plains of the Sava Dolinka, this charming town nestles between the massif of the Julian Alps in the west and the Karavanke range to the north. Two valleys radiate west from Bled, the Radovna and the Sava Bohinjska, each carving deep paths through the high wooded plateaus of Mežakla, Pokljuka and Jelovica. Forested slopes rise from the shores of Bled's emerald lake with the snow-capped peaks beyond providing a dramatic scenic backdrop. On the fringe of the north-east shores of the lake stands an impressive sixteenth-century castle (now a museum) which overlooks the town. A small island forms the foundation for a Gothic church which completes the fairy-tale scene.

Bled is no stranger to tourism. Priests on pilgrimages to the little church in the fifteenth century returned to speak of the area's unique beauty. The thermal springs attracted visitors seeking cures from their ailments while others simply came to breath the clear mountain air. Improved rail and road links in the mid nineteenth century contributed to the area's notoriety and Bled soon became well known throughout Europe. To the present day it is still one of Slovenia's principle tourist centres and as such offers the visitor a full range of facilities including tourist information, bank, post office, hospital, police station, chemist, garages, shops, supermarkets and restaurants. The area is also rich in cultural and historic monuments as well as many special sites of natural interest. A multitude of accommodation is available including all categories of hotels and private rooms. The town also has a youth hostel (Bledec) as well as camping Zaka on the west shore of the lake and camping Šobec 3km to the south-east of the town.

Bled has two rail stations: Bled-Jezero on the west side of the lake on the main Munich-Trieste line and Lesce on the main line from Ljubljana. Each involves a short bus or taxi ride to the town centre.

Bled is on the main road route from Ljubljana with border crossings to Italy and Austria from the Sava Dolinka Valley.

Buses run hourly to both Ljubljana (via Lesce) and Bohinj. Hourly services also connect Lesce to Kranjska Gora.

Many sporting activities are catered for and the area has a network of waymarked local trails. The town makes an ideal centre for the walker to enjoy a pastoral introduction to the eastern corner of the Julian Alps. All walks from Bled are described from the main bus station in the centre of the town.

## WALK 1: CIRCULAR TOUR OF LAKE BLED (BLEJSKO JEZERO)

| | |
|---|---|
| *Maps:* | Bled Načrt Mesta (town map) (1:6,600) |
| | Bled & surroundings walking map (1:25,000) |
| | Julian Alps - East part (1:50,000), Triglav National Park (1:50,000) |
| *Walking Time:* | 1 hour 30 minutes |
| *Grading:* | Easy. A pleasant introductory walk to the area taking in the many sites that line the scenic lake. No difficulties. |
| *Highest Altitude:* | 604m (Bled Castle) |
| *Lowest Altitude:* | 475m |
| *Approx. Distance:* | 6km |

This easy walk provides a tranquil introduction to the Julian Alps and follows a route around the crystal clear waters of Lake Bled (Blejsko Jezero). There are many places of interest along the route including an art gallery, castle, bathing, fishing, boating and trips to the island to visit the ninth-century church. The walk is particularly beautiful in the early morning when the mist is floating on the still waters and, if coupled with visits to the various historic sites, can provide a gentle first day's introduction to the area.

THE WALK
The walk is described in a clockwise direction around the lake as

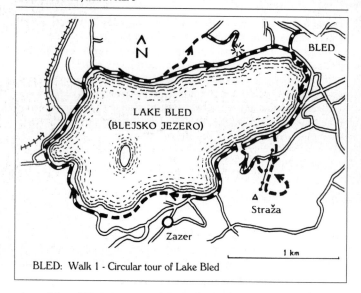

BLED: Walk 1 - Circular tour of Lake Bled

viewed from Bled. From the bus station in the centre of town walk down the Cesta Svobode towards the eastern shore of the lake and follow the path through the beautifully kept ornamental garden. The 144 hectare (365 acre) lake was formed by the retreat of the Bohinj glacier at the end of the last ice age and it is fed by underground springs that gives the water a very agreeable summer temperature of 24°C (75°F). Follow the shoreline past overhanging willow, beech and maple and beds of lilies, keeping an eye open for some of the many fish that cruise the shallows. The lake holds good specimens of coarse fish as well as trout, and fishing from the shore or from a boat is very popular with both visitors and locals. Rods can be hired locally and permits arranged by the tourist information office. Continue past the casino and the first of the four boat stations on the lake. The high peaks of the central massif can now be seen in the north-west. Pass the ivy-clad Grand Hotel Toplice where the path begins a short climb to reach the road.

A short deviation can be taken on the left to visit the summit of Straža (646m) which has good views down to the lake and across the wooded plateau of Pokljuka to Triglav. A chairlift operates daily

*The island church on Lake Bled*

throughout the summer from 0830 to 1900 and marked footpaths lead back to the lake shore.

Follow the road for a short way, deviating on a path that skirts the road tunnel to round a headland and arrive at the small village of Mlino. On the opposite side of the road is the Svetina Gallery, displaying interesting sculptures by Tone Svetina (admission free). Cross the small River Jezernica, which drains from the lake, and fork right at the bus station to continue by the shore line. Decorative wrought iron gates lead into the ground of the solubrious Hotel Villa Bled. Signs discourage swimming, fishing and flower picking. Continue into trees and pass steps leading up left to the Kavama Belvedere Cafe. The cafe balcony is positioned high above the trees and commands a magnificent view across the lake to Bled and beyond to the frontier ridge of the Karavanke mountains.

Emerge from the hotel grounds into a beautiful open glade dotted with beech and horse chestnut to join the road briefly before continuing along the lake shore on a wooden walkway. This section is particularly beautiful with views of the island church, Bled castle and the Karavanke mountains. Despite the close proximity of the

49

island to the western shore the full extent of the building work is still largely obscured by the dense vegetation growing on the small limestone plateau. It is not until the grand staircase that rises from the water has been climbed that the intricate nature of the building work can be appreciated. A pre-Romanesque chapel betrays man's early homage to this unique site. The church, chaplainry, staircase and the "bell of wishes" date from the early baroque period of the sixteenth century, and also boasts a lavish "golden altar" from the same period. The church is open daily from 0800 to 2000 and provides an atmospheric concert venue every Monday throughout the season.

The only way of reaching the island is by boat. Passengers are ferried to and fro in wooden craft that resemble canopied punts from four boat stations positioned around the lake (70din return trip). For those who feel they could do with the extra exercise rowing boats are also available for hire.

The walkway continues around to an inlet on the west side of the lake that has been developed to cater for watersports. Many people come to spectate or compete here in the popular May Day rowing regatta. Across the road to the left is the entrance to the lakeside campsite (Zaka).

Follow the path around right to continue along the water's edge to reach the Zaka rowing club. By the water is a bust of Boris Kocjančič erected by club members in memory of the founder and longtime president of the only rowing club in Slovenia. A short distance away stands an impressive statue of boatmen, created between the first and second world wars by Boris Kalin.

Continue along the shore, now shaded under the wooded slopes of Višce to below the castle cliffs. A path rising into the trees on the left leads up to the castle (signposted GRAD 1). The castle was built on the edge of a rock precipice almost 100m above the lake. Excavations have shown that fortifications existed here as far back as Roman times, but the earliest buildings preserved today date back to the Middle Ages. Various buildings were added through the years and the present day architecture dates largely from the sixteenth century. A fire destroyed large sections of the roofings in 1947 and extensive restoration by architect Tone Bitenc took place between 1951 and 1961. The castle is now protected as a museum and commands a view that befits its once valued strategic position.

Keep to the lakeside to pass the Triglav National Park Information Centre which has all kinds of information on the park and is well worth a visit (open 1000 to 1600). From the information centre continue past a bathing area where a section of the lake has been roped off to provide swimming facilities. Sunbeds are also available for hire. Return to the lake shore once again and reach the starting point at the eastern end of the lake.

## WALK 2: BLED - VINTGAR GORGE - ST KATERINA - BLED

| | |
|---|---|
| *Maps:* | Bled & surroundings walking map (1:25,000) |
| | Julian Alps - East part (1:50,000), Triglav National Park (1:50,000) |
| *Walking Time:* | 3¹/₂ - 4 hours |
| *Grading:* | Easy/Moderate. Well waymarked trail. All sections of footpath within the gorge are well protected. Wooden walkway can be slippery when wet. |
| *Highest Altitude:* | 634m |
| *Lowest Altitude:* | 501m |
| *Approx. Distance:* | 10.5km |

The Vintgar gorge, situated to the north-west of Bled, is a dramatic example of the effect of water erosion on the limestone bedrock. The channel, which is several hundred metres deep in places, has been sculpted over many centuries by the relentless action of the Radovna river draining the waters of the high mountains to the open Sava plains. The walk passes through the small agricultural settlements of Podhom, Zasip and Mužje, where traditional farming methods are still in evidence, and returns to Bled across the open grassland of the Gorenjsko plains.

THE WALK
Leave Bled heading north-west on the Grajska Cesta, forking right to pass the library before joining the main Prešernova Cesta. Follow

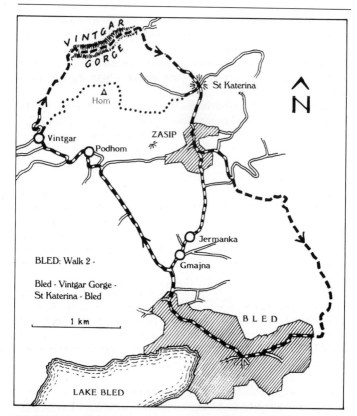

BLED: Walk 2 -

Bled - Vintgar Gorge -
St Katerina - Bled

this for about 200m before forking right again onto the Partizanska
Cesta. Open fields quickly begin to dominate the foreground and
the ever present ridge of the Karavanke suddenly appears more
imposing in its grandure.

Cross the small Rečica stream and take the next left turning
(signposted Podhom). Follow the small roadway for about 1¹/₂km
through avenues of oak and flower choked meadows stretching out
in either direction. To the west, above the tree covered plateau of
Pokljuka, rise the jagged peaks of the Julian Alps while to the east
the mountains of the Karavanke compete for attention.

On reaching the hamlet of Podhom turn left under a stone rail bridge and continue straight on following signs to Vintgar. Follow the road around to the right through a maze of typically charming cottages with cascades of colour spilling from the carved wooden balconies and small gardens ablaze with an overwhelming multitude of flowers.

At the end of the street turn left and continue past a small roadside shrine to the Virgin Mary, ignoring signs to Gorje. The track now begins to ascend along a shaded lane of overhanging beech and levels, with further views of rolling pastures to the left. Turn right following signs to Vintgar along a track lined with rhododendron to reach a T-junction.

An alternative route that by-passes the gorge may be taken at this junction by turning sharp right (signposted Hom). The small path ascends gently at first across open meadows before climbing thickly wooded slopes to reach the summit of Hom (834m). The summit offers a magnificent view over Bled and the Gorenjsko plains. A path then descends from the summit to join the described route at the church of St Katerina.

Turn right at the T-junction and begin descending around a sharp dog-leg to cross the Radovna River and enter the Triglav National Park boundary downstream of the bridge. Car parking space is available either side of the road and a Tourist Bus service operates three times a day between the gorge entrance and Bled (times are displayed on a blue sign at all stopping points). Continue along the road to a small wooden refreshment bar that marks the entrance to the gorge. The entrance fee helps to pay for the upkeep of the wooden galleries, bridges and walkways that have been constructed along the base of the steep cliffs.

A path begins to descend steep wooded slopes to reach the entrance to the gorge at a bridge. Cross this and continue along the far bank beneath the steepening rock walls. Continue along the walkways into the cool depths of the 1km channel crossing and recrossing the river. The river passes through a series of rapids interspersed with deep turquoise pools holding stocks of trout that can be seen rising for food in the slack water. At the third crossing of the river the gorge is at its deepest and narrowest and from this point begins to open out to reach the Sum Falls below the stone rail

bridge suspended above the deep channel. A restaurant is situated at the far end of the gorge selling drinks, refreshments and souvenirs.

Signposts to Bled lead up by a series of steps into a wood which has an eerie silence compared to the water thundering echos of the gorge. The path meanders through trees to level briefly at an open glade before continuing through open pasture and shaded wood to ascend a bouldery stream bed which leads through further meadows and out of the National Park boundary to the gothic church of St Katerina. The new restaurant detracts from the tranquillity of the spot but the view across the Gorenjsko plain is quite magnificent.

From St Katerina continue straight ahead on a track, following signs to Bled, and descend into the village of Zasip with its fine thirteenth-century church. From the village two alternatives are available. The first is to continue on to the small hamlet of Gmajna, crossing the Rečica stream to enter Bled on the main Prešernova Cesta. But a far more pleasant return route is to take the second turning on the left from the village passing through the settlement of Mužje to reach a T-junction at the first hairpin along the track. Turn left and follow a faint track across open meadow for about 100m before taking another track off left into woods. Take the next turning right to follow a fenceline on the fringe of woods with beautiful open pasture to the right. Continue straight ahead at a fork ignoring a path that follows the forest edge on the left and join the crest of a high embankment until the track swings sharp right into the suburbs of Bled. Keeping generally straight ahead follow the winding road through the houses to cross the Rečica River and join the Ljubljana Cesta. Turn right and right again at the Hotel Krim to join the Prešernova Cesta which leads back to the bus station and the starting point of the walk.

*Walkways around Vintgar Gorge*

## WALK 3: BLED - KORITNO - BODEŠČE - LOVSKA KOČA
## TALEŽU - RIBNO - BLED

| | |
|---|---|
| *Maps:* | Bled & surroundings walking map (1:25,000) |
| | Julian Alps - East part (1:50,000), Triglav National Park (1:50,000) |
| *Walking Time:* | 5 hours 30 minutes |
| *Grading:* | Moderate. Although no sections of the route has any technical difficulties the forest path is steep in a few sections. Waymarking is adequate but care is required in places. |
| *Highest Altitude:* | 700m |
| *Lowest Altitude:* | 421m |
| *Approx. Distance:* | 14km |

To the south of Bled lie the forested slopes of Jelovica. The area is a vast plateau of limestone riddled with hollows, swallow holes and other Karst features that are characteristic of the Julian Alps. The height of the plateau varies between 1,000 and 1,100m and the region is thickly wooded. This walk crosses the pastures of the Gorenjsko plain to reach the lower slopes of Jelovica, rising from the southern bank of the beautiful Sava Bohinjka River before climbing steeply to the hunting lodge at Talež and a magnificent viewpoint. The path is then followed to return to Bled through the pretty village of Ribno.

THE WALK
Leave the centre of Bled east on the main road (Ljubljana Cesta). Continue along this road to reach the outskirts of the town where another road descends to the right. Follow this across a bridge and after 200m take a road to the right and begin ascending. The road begins to level on reaching the small hamlet of Koritno and continues past the collection of modern chalets to reach a hairpin where a track descends to the left (signposted Šobec). The track descends quite steeply into an area of open pastureland that is characteristic of the Gorenjsko plain where small barns and the uniquely designed racks

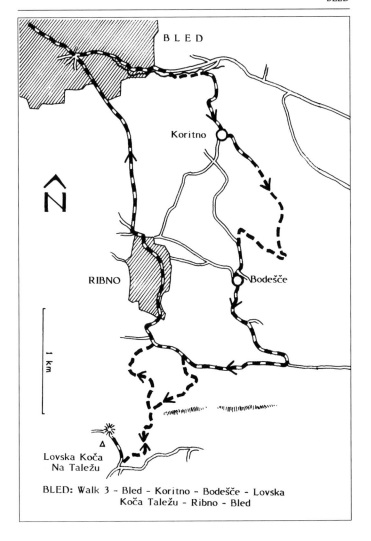

BLED: Walk 3 - Bled - Koritno - Bodešče - Lovska
Koča Taležu - Ribno - Bled

for drying hay - called *Kozolec* - litter the open meadows. Cows peacefully grazing on the carpet of grass and flowers add to the serenity of the scene.

The track passes a small barn on the left and after a further 100m enters the cover of trees. Take the next right fork which leads out into pasture, crossing a stream before reaching a copse of trees. Begin climbing on a faint path keeping right to join a track. Turn right and begin to ascend the shingle surface, turning left at a T-junction to reach a road. Follow signs to Bodešče along a surfaced road which undulates past farmsteads and orchards to arrive at the small hamlet.

At a junction marked by a religious shrine turn left following signs to Sava (river) and follow the narrow road as it swings around to the right passing a pretty collection of farm buildings. The iridescent water of the Sava can be seen sparkling in the sunlight below with the tree covered slopes beyond rising to the Jelovica plateau. The ornate gothic spire of the fifteenth-century church of St Lenart comes into view directly ahead rising above the tree covered plateau on which it was built. A road to Na Skali leads off left to the church which contains an interesting mid fifteenth-century fresco of St George in combat with a dragon. Continue the descent passed alpine chalets decorated with colourful stone wall rockeries and follow beneath a precipitous cliff wall on the left to reach the Sava Bohinjka. Close inspeciton of rock wall reveals the tiny aluminium bolts used by rock climbers indicating this to be a popular climbing venue.

The bridge across the river provides a wonderful viewpoint north across the wooded foothills of Mežakla to the peaks of the central Julian Alps. Cross the bridge and turn right to follow a good path. Ignore tracks running off right and left but continue along the path which widens to pass a summer pasture camp before opening out to reveal a splendid panorama of the Julian and Karavanke mountain ranges. Reach a path junction and fork left on a track that swings around left passing another summer pasture camp before veering right to enter the forest. The walk can be shortened by continuing past the initial left fork and remaining on the main path which will shortly join the return route of the described walk at the Ribenski *most* (bridge) river crossing. The return trip to the hunting

*Hunting lodge at Lovska Talez*

lodge at Taležu takes about $1^{1}/_{2}$ to 2 hours.

Having entered the forest the rugged path now follows around a series of hairpins and begins to gain height gently with occasional detours to avoid small rock outcrops. Cross a stream bed before veering around right to a short steep section that leads to a path junction. Take the left fork and continue the ascent, zig-zagging over bouldery rock to negotiate numerous rock barriers. A final steep section is climbed before the tree canopy begins to open and the path emerges to join a wide track at the site of a war memorial. Turn right and continue for 100m before turning right again at the junction with another track and follow this easily to reach the Lovska Koča in a few minutes.

The small hunter's lodge provides refreshments and a balcony at which to sit and view the magnificent panorama. The Karavanke range dominates the north-east with its serrated ridge and cascades of scree falling to the open plains below. To the west rise the Julian Alps above the Pokljuka forests. Lake Bled is partially obscured by the 646m peak of Straža but the small town of Ribno and the return route of the walk can be seen clearly below.

Retrace the route of ascent to the small memorial and descend the rock strewn track back into the forest. After two zig-zags turn left at a path junction and after a further 100m follow a small path right which descends through the forest on the left side of a deep ravine. The path negotiates a series of small rock steps and outcrops winding down steeply into the bed of the ravine. Cross a small stream and continue past a path intersection following a sign to Bled. Reach a section of open meadow lined with evergreen and take a right fork which leads to a junction with a forest track. Continue directly ahead through a lightly wooded section to emerge with views across to the church at Bodešče, at Ribenski *most*, the bridge crossing the Sava Bohinjka.

Cross the river and follow a shingle track which climbs gently into the village of Ribno. The street is lined with all manner of alpine cottages, chalets and barns each decorated with stunning arrangements of flowers as if in competition for the attention of the visitor. Turn left at the T-junction and continue to another road junction where the route turns left to reach a crossroads. Turn right and after a few metres right again to follow the road through open fields dotted with wooded *kozolecs*. The Karavanke mountains dominate the view ahead with the small peaks of Dobra Gora (620m) and Straža (646m) to the west. The castle stands sentinel above the town of Bled which is soon reached after about 2km. The road joins the Ljubljana Cesta which is followed to the town centre.

## WALK 4: BLED - HOTUNJSKI VTH (1,107m) - ZATRNIK - KRNICA - BLED

| | |
|---|---|
| *Maps:* | Bled & surroundings walking map (1:25,000) |
| | Julian Alps - East part (1:50,000), Triglav National Park (1:50,000) |
| *Walking Time:* | 7 hours |
| *Grading:* | Difficult. A hard forest walk with some route finding difficulties. Sections of the walk are overgrown and steep. Infrequent waymarking means a map and compass is essential. An altimeter may also prove useful although not essential. |

| | |
|---|---|
| *Highest Altitude:* | 1,107m |
| *Lowest Altitude:* | 475m |
| *Approx. Distance:* | 9km - Zatrnik, 12.5km - Krnica, 17.5km - Bled. |

The route climbs the wooded foothills of the Pokljuka plateau, gaining height through remote glades and clearings in some of the most beautiful forest in the area. The walk provides an opportunity to view the flora and fauna of this undisturbed habitat. Deer, hare, fox and squirrels are common residents as are grouse, eagle, buzzard and woodpeckers. The path climbs to reach Hotunjski Vth at 1,107m from where there is an unparalleled panorama of the area. Return is via the small ski resort of Zatrnik from where transport can be arranged back to Bled or the walk can be continued on foot through a series of beautiful villages.

THE WALK

From the centre of Bled walk down to the eastern shores of the lake. Follow the water's edge around to the right until the path ascends behind the boat hire station to join the road. Cross the road and continue ascending on a small wooded path (signposted Višce - 2; the number refers to local routes highlighted on the local walking map). The path emerges at an open meadow, which is popular with picnickers, before descending to cross a deep cut depression. Continue straight ahead contouring the southern slopes of Višce on an undulating course with glimpses through the trees to the waters of Lake Bled below on the left. The path swings around to the right with views across left to the chalets of Nad Progo nestled beneath the steep forested slopes that the route will ascend, before climbing steeply to emerge from the trees. Continue sheepishly through private gardens to cross the Rečica stream over a small stone bridge to the left and turn right onto the road which leads to a T-junction. Continue left and follow the road around until it's possible to make a right turning under a stone rail bridge, following signs to Kuhovnica and Stan-4. At a crossroads turn left and after 100m take a rubble strewn track forking to the right.

The track begins to ascend into the forest waymarked periodically by the number 4 which offers reassurance. Pass a good viewpoint on the left back to Lake Bled and continue directly ahead ignoring a

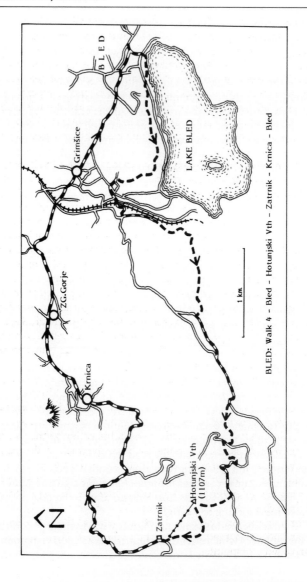

BLED: Walk 4 - Bled - Hotunjski Vth - Zatrnik - Krnica - Bled

track forking right. The path levels occasionally on its upward course to cross open glades of grass and fern decorated with an abundance of delicate wild flowers. At an open section of fenced meadow watch out for an unlikely left turning. Continue through trees before emerging to cross a small open glade of heather. Re-enter the forest, turning right to pass another good viewpoint down to Lake Bled, before descending slightly to join a motorable track in more open ground. Turning right at this junction will lead back to the crossroads at Na Logo from where the route can be reversed to Bled.

Turn left and follow the track which forms part of the local route 15 - waymarking to that effect appears periodically. After a short distance the track begins to steepen. Ignore another track leading off left at this point but follow around sharply to the right to reach a hairpin bend 100m further on. Leave the track on the right to cross a meadow trending slightly left and ascend towards an old wooded chalet on no distinct path. Continue the ascent to the right of the chalet in a rubbly stream bed (waymark on rock). Follow this steeply to pass another chalet on the left and the last of the waymarking to reach a fork. Take the right turn and follow a faint, overgrown path to reach a forest track. Turn right and follow this to join a higher track at an open section of pasture by a small chalet. If, for any reason walkers wish to abandon the described route this track can be followed to the right and will, in about 2km, join with the main Zatrnik-Krnica road.

To continue ascend a faint path behind the chalet which soon widens to a track and under a high canopy of beech. The path veers to the left, meandering around the boulder strewn forest floor and continues ascending to emerge at another track. Turn right and begin descending slightly with views of the valley on the left. At a corner by a disused barn on the left leave the track on the right to climb a short, steep grassy mound that soon leads into a small glade. Cross the clearing to exit on the right and enter tree cover before veering left to emerge on the edge of a winter ski run. Turn right and begin to climb the steep, grassy slope by trees lining the right edge. After a steep climb reach a ski lift and ascend the rocky mound behind to reach the summit of Hotunjski Vrh (1,107m) and an unrivalled viewpoint.

The summit commands an unforgettable view of this region of the Julian Alps. To the west stretches the Pokljuka plateau with the rocky spires of the central peaks beyond. To the north the Radovna Valley carves its course through the forested hills and beyond rise the peaks of the frontier border with Austria. Ahead the Gorenjsko plains stretch across to the peaks of the Karavanke with Lake Bled shining like a jewel in the valley basin.

Return to the ski lift and begin descending the steep grass slope to its left (looking down). If the grass is either wet or covered with late snow safer progress may be made by keeping close to the wooded sections that fringe the slope. At the foot of the steep section turn right and continue descending more easily on a track to join the road at the developing winter resort of Zatrnik.

The exploitation of the mountains for downhill skiing often results in wholesale destruction of the environment but the resort of Zatrnik, small by most European standards, has managed to develop the surrounding slopes without destroying any of the natural charm of the landscape. Refreshments are available in the pretty town where a taxi may be arranged to the bus stop at Krnica. Alternatively the walk to Krnica is not unpleasant and offers some impressive views left to the cliffs of the Pokijuska Soteska gorge.

Buses run twice daily from Krnica to Bled. Times are displayed at the Bled bus station. The walk may be continued through the village of Zg. Gorje, Sp. Gorje, Grimšice and on to Bled. The route is about 8½km and makes a pleasant way of finishing off the outing.


## WALK 5: BLED - MALA OSOJNICA (685m) - VELIKA OSOJNICA (756m) - OJSTRICA (610m) - BLED

*Maps:*     Bled Načrt Mesta (1:6,600)

        Bled & surroundings walking map (1:25,000)

        Julian Alps - East part (1:50,000), Triglav National Park (1:50,000)

*Near the Summit of Triglav. Photo: G.Sellers*

Jalovec seen from near the summit of Prisojnik (M & T Leafe)
Statue to the first men to climb Triglav (Author)

| | |
|---|---|
| *Walking Time:* | 3¹/₂ hours |
| *Grading:* | Moderate. Well waymarked route. The path is steep and rugged in parts. All exposed sections are well protected. |
| *Highest Altitude:* | 756m |
| *Lowest Altitude:* | 475m |
| *Approx. Distance:* | 8.5km |

There is a popular belief that size is not a measure of quality and that is certainly the case with this delightful walk. The route ascends a well prepared path to visit three summits situated on the far side of Lake Bled. Each summit is very different in character but all offer magnificent views over Lake Bled and the surrounding countryside. The walk can be combined with Walk 1, although its quality can certainly justify an independent outing. The beauty of this walk lies not only in the marvellous views but also in the enchanting atmosphere on a meandering route beneath a high tree canopy.

THE WALK
Follow the route description for Walk 1 along the southern shores of Lake Bled until the road is joined at the south-west corner of the lake on emerging from the grounds of the Hotel Villa Bled. Take a path leading off sharp left from the road by a seat (signposted Mala Osojnica - 6). Climb a set of steep steps, zig-zagging left before entering the forest above a large alpine chalet. The route tends to be

BLED: Walk 5 - Bled - Mala Osojnica - Velika Osojnica - Ojstrica - Bled

rather over enthusiastically waymarked with the number 6 liberally decorating every available tree trunk along the path.

Height is gained rapidly, the path climbing through a series of well graded zig-zags before swinging left to avoid what appears to be an insurmountable barrier of rock. The forested slope falls

65

steeply from the edge of the path and is pleasantly exposed in places. A small rock step leads back to the base of the cliff where an iron stairway, built in 1976, overcomes the obstacle in eighty-eight ever steepening steps. A handrail is provided and offers a welcome feeling of security in the top section. The steps emerge at a stunning viewpoint down to the lake where the intricate nature of the building work on the island can be appreciated.

The path continues to ascend from behind the seat in another series of zig-zags before levelling with glimpses left of Lake Bled framed by overhanging branches of beech. Descend slightly before climbing again over rock and roots to another viewpoint of the lake below the wooded summit of Mala Osojnica. The path continues through the fairy-tale forest carpeted in leaves to reach an indistinct fork, where a short detour left leads to a good viewpoint south across the Jelovica and Pokljuka plateaus and the deep channel of the Sava Bohinjka Valley.

Rejoin the path and continue descending slightly before veering left. Ignore a path descending left to the town of Bohinjska Bela but continue to ascend through an enchanting section of wood. Negotiate a series of small rocky outcrops before finally climbing in zig-zags to the tree shrouded summit of Velika Osojnica (756m). The path continues across the summit, turning left to descend a bouldery slope to reach a viewpoint east across the lake to the Karavanke mountains beyond.

Retrace the route across the summit of Velika Osojnica and continue descending into the forest depression between Velika Osojnica and Mala Osojnica to reach the junction of three paths. Turn left and begin descending on a small path which, after a few metres, widens to a large rubble strewn track. Descend this steeply to a small glade where the angle relents and the path continues on a pleasant meandering course. Don't miss a turning left (signposted Ojstrica) to follow a route ascending to a small cliff of rock. The path continues over easy rock steps to reach the rocky summit of Ojstrica (610m) with fine views across the lake.

From the summit retrace the route down to join the main track and continue the descent until emerging from the forest beside a small pasture. Reach a motorable track which leads easily down to the lakeside.

From the water's edge follow either bank around the lake to return to Bled (see Walk 1 description).

## WALK 6: BLED - BOHINJSKA BELA - KUPLJENIK - BLED

| | |
|---|---|
| *Maps:* | Bled & surroundings walking map (1:25,000) |
| | Julian Alps - East part (1:50,000), Triglav National Park (1:50,000) |
| *Walking Time:* | 5 hours |
| *Grading:* | Easy / Moderate. Well waymarked path with no particular difficulties. The ascent from Bohinjska Bela to Kupljenik is a bit of a slog. |
| *Highest Altitude:* | 650m |
| *Lowest Altitude:* | 468m |
| *Approx. Distance:* | 15km |

This beautiful walk explores the pastures of the Sava Bohinjka and visits the small town of Bohinjska Bela at the northern end of the ravine formed by the steep cliffs of Pokljuka and Jelovica. The route then crosses the river, ascending to the quaint hamlet of Kupljenik to traverse an area of beautiful upland pasture before descending to recross the river by the village of Log. The return route follows an interesting path that cuts between the peaks of Straža and Dobra Gora before finally descending back into Bled.

THE WALK

Begin along the south shores of Lake Bled (see Walk 1) and reach the small stone bridge that crosses the Jezernica stream at the hamlet of Mlino. Begin ascending the road before turning left to descend a narrow surfaced track opposite the entrance to the Hotel Villa Bled. The track reaches the pretty village of Zazer and continues past flower decked chalets to a junction. Turn left (signposted Bohinj Bela - 5) and begin descending to pass a woodyard on the left. A crucifix marks the next junction where a track rising to the right is followed to rejoin the main Bled - Bohinj road. Turn left and follow the road for 100m before taking a faint track leading off from a

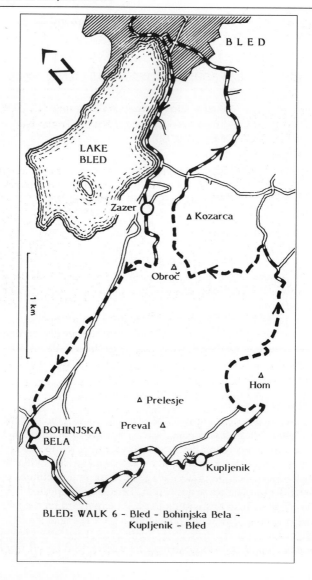

BLED: WALK 6 – Bled – Bohinjska Bela –
Kupljenik – Bled

*Seventeenth-century church of St Marjete at Bohinjska Bela
with cliffs of Bibji Zob behind*

gravel lay-by on the right. Immediately enter open pasture and
continue towards the town of Bohinj Bela following the edge of the
forest on the right, passing small barns and numerous *kozolecs*.

The deep cut ravine of the Bohinjska Valley and the precipitous
cliffs of Babji Zob (old woman's tooth) can be seen directly ahead as
the path passes small cultivated plots to enter Bohinjska Bela. The
town is built on a series of rising terraces beneath the eastern cliffs
of Pokljuka with the seventeenth-century church of St Marjeta
forming an impressive centrepiece. Bohinjska Bela was for many
centuries the last settlement of the valley that was still accessible
from Bled. Communication links through the steep sided ravine to
Bohinj were poor from this direction and, until the construction of
the road, consisted only of a small footpath.

Turn right and cross the River Belica, from which the town
derived its name, to a crossroads. Buses run hourly from this point

to and from Bled. A short detour can be made by continuing straight ahead at the crossroads into Zgornja (upper) Bela to visit the 25m high Iglico waterfall, but to continue the walk turn left following the first and last sign to Kupljenik. Descend through a series of pretty cottages to cross the Sava Bohinjka where the road swings around right to join the main road from Bled to Bohinj at a crossroad.

Cross this and begin ascending on a surfaced track that meanders wildly to gain height through rolling pasture lined with fruit trees. The silence is only broken by the scampering of squirrels in the branches, the chatter of birds and the occasional chiming of bells as the cows graze the open meadows.

The village of Kupljenik appears quite suddenly, its quaint wooden cottages and barns decked in trailing vine and lavished with geraniums. The track now becomes unsurfaced and climbs to reach the church of St Stefana. Continue along the track, ascending slightly to reach an open balcony that traverses rolling meadows with glorious open views over the Gorenjsko plain and the mountains of the Karavanke. In the foreground the twin peaks of Straža and Dobra Gora, between which the return route will pass, obscure the lake and castle at Bled.

This delightful position lasts until the track swings left between rickety barns and begins to descend past a small farmstead. Continue descending to reach open pastures and a small religious monument and leave the main track to descend directly along the right edge of the pasture, passing through a collection of fruit trees and aiming for a small shed where a path leads off right past a lonely gravestone into forest. The path contours the northern slopes of Mt Hom, with waymarking for route 11 now appearing intermittently on tree trunks, before descending around small rock walls and loose rocky steps to reach a fenceline. Follow this on easier ground until the Sava Bohinjka comes into sight.

Cross the river at the wooden bridge (*Selski most*) and take an obvious track to the left just before reaching the village of Log. An alternative to this would be to continue through Log to reach Selo Pri Bledu where a left turn leads to the southern shore of Lake Bled through the village of Mlino, or continue straight ahead to reach Bled via the village of Želeče.

To continue the walk follow the track left with views back to the slopes of Gradisce. Ignore a first track leading right but take a second after 50m at the junction of three tracks, heading directly for the wooded mound of Obroč. The track begins to climb slightly to reach a crossroads. Turn right and after 20m continue straight ahead at another intersection to follow a shaded track. Begin to climb once more with views of Bled Castle and the Karavanke to arrive at a crossroads in the centre of Mlino. A left turn leads shortly to Lake Bled but continue straight ahead on an unlikely looking road until a track can be seen climbing behind a newly built guest house. Follow this track, which is a little overgrown in parts, until an area of scree is reached falling from the southern slops of Straža and marking the saddle between the two peaks of Straža and Dobra Gora.

Continue down the narrow path to reach the open pasture of Gorenjsko and follow around left on the edge of tree cover to emerge finally into one of Bled's more stylish and colourful suburbs. At the end of the street a signpost left beckons to the summit of Straža but if the call is unheard continue on the main road which is followed easily back to the centre of Bled.

# BOHINJ

Bohinj (523m) is the collective name given to the string of settlements along the Sava Bohinjka Valley and includes: Bohinjska Bela, Nomenj, Bohinjska Bistrica, Ribčev Laz and Stara Fužina. At the head of the valley is Lake Bohinj (Bohinjsko Jezero) - the pearl of Slovenia and undoubtedly one of the most beautiful lakes in the country. Bounded on the south-side by the lower Bohinj mountain range, to the north by the plateau of Fužinarska Visoravan and to the west the precipitous headwall of Komarča the lake is indeed impressively sited. The area is within the Triglav National Park boundary and is considerably less developed than Bled, giving nature a free rein to parade its splendours. Despite the many visitors, Bohinj manages to maintain the atmosphere of a secluded beauty spot, making it one of the most idyllic settings in the Julian Alps.

The tides of change that swept over Slovenia in early history went largely unnoticed in this remote corner of the mountains and the lifestyle of the inhabitants was relatively unchanged. The smelting of iron was the basis for Bohinj life for many centuries until increased competition throughout Europe, especially from cheap English iron, closed the last of the Bohinj smelteries at the turn of the century. The agriculture in the valley has always centred around livestock, the people making a modest living growing potatoes, beans and maize to keep themselves and the cattle through the hard winters. The same methods of farming are used today with traditional Bohinj cheese still being made in the high pastures during the summer months.

The rail connection into Bohinjska Bistrica not only brought with it a new source of employment but also an increase in tourism. People came to marvel at the Lake and to walk in the hills and pastures. Many of the local men, experienced in the mountains, offered their services as guides and actively promoted the area as a popular base for ascents of Mt Triglav, which it has remained to this day. With improved road connections to Bled the main tourist centre moved from Bohinjska Bistrica to its present position by the Lake at Ribčev Laz.

Accommodation is plentiful with a number of B class hotels, private rooms, a youth hostel and an idyllic campsite on the western lake shore at Ukanc. Facilities available include tourist information, post office, supermarket, garage, shops and restaurants. Prices are generally cheaper here than the more commercially orientated centre of Bled. A cable car and chairlifts operate throughout the summer from the village of Ukanc, taking visitors to a combined height of almost 1,800m onto the lower slopes of the Mt Vogel mountain ridge. Bohinjska Bistrica is on the main Munich-Trieste rail line but visitors tavelling from Ljubljana will find it easier to connect with one of the hourly buses that run between the Lake and Bled. The only reasonable road connection is also via Bled.

Walks in the area visit many natural spectacles and local trails are waymarked. Walks described in this guide start and finish by the lakeside at Ribčev Laz.

## WALK 1: CIRCULAR TOUR OF LAKE BOHINJ (BOHINJSKO JEZERO)

| | |
|---|---|
| *Maps:* | Panoramic map of Bohinj, Julain Alps - Bohinj (1:20,000) |
| | Julian Alps - East part (1:50,000), Triglav National Park (1:50,000) |
| *Walking Time:* | 3 - 4 hours |
| *Grading:* | Easy. Adequate waymarking along a good path that follows easily around the lake shore. |
| *Highest Altitude:* | 540m |
| *Lowest Altitude:* | 525m |
| *Approx. Distance:* | 12km |

This walk presents an easy but delightfully pleasant introduction to the Bohinj Valley. Larger than Lake Bled the lake at Bohinj was formed at the head of the Bohinj glacial valley during the last ice age.

The lake once covered much of the upper Bohinj Valley until the Sava Bohinjka established its course, draining the water to its present level. It is just under 4.5km long, over 1km wide and covers an area of over 3.25sq.km making it the largest lake in Slovenia. In an effort to preserve its natural beauty building is forbidden on the shoreline and motorboats are banned from the water.

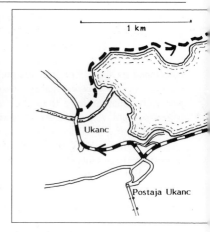

THE WALK

From the stone bridge that spans the Sava Bohinjka follow the road that runs along the southern shore signposted Savica. A small boathouse on the right hires kayaks and windsurfers and to the left, set back from the road, is a steep limestone cliff where local climbers can be seen strenuously inching their way up the vertical rock. Early morning jogging appears to have been surpassed in popularity, even in summer, by cross country skiing. Short lengths of wood with conventional bindings and small wheels act as substitute skis and the roadway around the lake is a popular circuit for local devotees.

Follow the path that runs alongside the road, which lessens the risk of an unfortunate encounter with motor vehicle or skier, and continue past the Hotel Pod Voglom. Boats are available for hire by the shore and seats are thoughtfully provided for non participants who simply want to take in the stunning scenery around the lake.

The path soon reaches the church of St Duh (church of the holy spirit) set back from the lake on the left. The church dates from the sixteenth century and was built to commemorate a bad harvest and resulting starvation in the area. The exterior is adorned with a charming fresco of St Christopher.

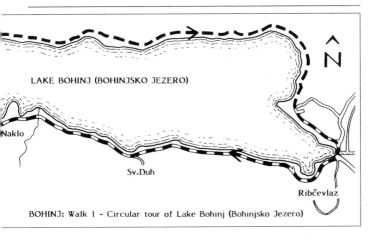

LAKE BOHINJ (BOHINJSKO JEZERO)

Naklo

Sv.Duh

Ribčevlaz

BOHINJ: Walk I - Circular tour of Lake Bohinj (Bohinjsko Jezero)

The road leaves the water's edge at the Naklova Glava headland where numerous tracks lead down to the lake, providing good photographic opportunities back to Stara Fužina and the Ribnica Valley. The scenery around the lake is a test for anybody's photographic skills with its grand scale and dramatic lighting contrasts defying all attempts to reproduce the spectacle into print.

The road can be left at this point to follow a track that runs alongside the water's edge to re-emerge at a crossroads. Turn right and continue along the road past the entrance to the idyllically positioned campsite and through a section of open pasture to reach the village of Ukanc. Buses run hourly calling at all stops to Bled from opposite the Hotel Zlatorog in the centre of the village.

Continue past the hotel to cross the emerald waters of the Savica by a wooden bridge and take a track right (signposted Stara Fužina, Ribčev Laz - 2 hours). Cross a small area of meadow and turn left to emerge at an open expanse of grassland sloping gently to the water's edge. The shallow water can reach up to 23°C in summer and the area is popular for bathing. Rowing boats are also available for hire.

Continue around the inlet to enter the forest which stretches down to the lakeside and traverse tongues of scree cascading down from the cliffs of Pršivec. The proximity of the cliffs imparts an impressive sense of scale with the rock strata twisted and broken by the awesome forces of nature.

The path leaves the water's edge to shortcut a headland from where the Govic waterfall can be seen to the left in the Pršivec cliffs. The cliffs contain a hidden lake in a cavern some distance above the surface of the Lake Bohinj and the two are connected via an underground stream. During the spring thaws or after heavy periods of rain the cavern becomes flooded with an excess of water draining from the higher valleys and the excess is ejected from a spout in the cliff face, cascading 100m before draining into the lake. The headland was formed by the debris washed down from this violent eruption.

Cross a boulder strewn channel that runs down to the lake and pass alpine chalets before returning to the water's edge. The cliff line to the left begins to receed and the path follows a meandering course around boulders with good views across to Stara Fužina. The shoreline has taken on an almost tropical appearance with bleached shingle gently sloping into the clear turquoise water. The path passes a trout fishery with numerous cylindrical concrete holding pools containing fish in various stages of maturity, prior to their release into the lake or sale to local restaurants.

The path now widens to a track bordered on the left by open meadows, to reach the inlet on the north-eastern shore with good views across to the serrated ridge of the lower Bohinj mountains. Continue along the shore backed by open grassland to reach a roadhead by the Kopališče café. Follow this under a tree canopy to a track leading down to the lakeside on the right and rejoin the road at the church of St John the Baptist. The church stands on an old religious site dating back to the time when missionaries were active in the area, gaining converts to Christianity. The present church was built in the fourteenth to fifteenth centuries, the oldest parts being Romanesque. The fan vaulting is from the late Gothic period and the baroque bell tower dates from 1738. Fourteenth-century frescoes adorn both interior and exterior while the beautiful altar was a more recent eighteenth-century addition. The church is considered to be one of the most important cultural monuments in Gorenjska.

Turn left to cross the Sava Bohinjka at the stone bridge into

*Church of St John the Baptist at Ribčev Laz*

Ribčev Laz. On the left, opposite the tourist information office, stands a bronze sculpture by Stojan Batic of the first men to reach the summit of Triglav.

## WALK 2: UKANC - SLAP SAVICA (SAVICA WATERFALL) - UKANC

| | |
|---|---|
| *Maps:* | Panoramic map of Bohinj, Julian Alps - Bohinj (1:20,000) |
| | Julian Alps - East part (1:50,000), Triglav National Park (1:50,000) |
| *Walking Time:* | 2¹/₂ - 3 hours. |
| *Grading:* | Easy. Well waymarked prepared footpath throughout. |
| *Highest Altitude:* | 767m |
| *Lowest Altitude:* | 654m |
| *Approx. Distance:* | 8.5km |

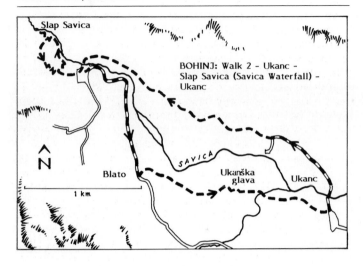

One of the main tourist attractions at Bohinj has unfortunately become a little over commercialised, the ease of access somewhat decrying a unique natural phenomena. Nevertheless the Savica waterfall is spectacular enough not to miss. The walk begins at the bus station at Ukanc and follows a good track to Koča pri Savici where a prepared set of steps climbs the 113m of vertical height to the falls. A pleasant return route through forest and open meadows leads back to Ukanc. Buses run from Ribčev Laz regularly throughout the day to the bus station outside the Hotel Zlatorog in Ukanc. Alternatively the route may be combined with a tour of the lake (Walk 1) to give a more lengthy outing.

THE WALK

From the Hotel Zlatorog cross the Savica River by a wooden bridge and continue along the gravel track passing a collection of Alpine chalets. The track swings around sharply to the left but continue ahead on a smaller path (signposted Slap Savica 1 hour). Cross a small stone bridge and continue along the gently ascending path lined with spruce. Cross a large pipe delivering water to the obscured electricity station on the left to reach an ornate wooden waymark giving distance and direction to all major European cities. London is supposably 1,200km further along the path!

The path begins to narrow and becomes more rugged as it continues the gentle ascent past regular waymarks and signs to the falls. Although still some distance away the roar of the water can already be heard, amplified by the towering cliff at the valley head. The Savica River presently comes into view at the base of a deep ravine to the left. Pass a path leading into the forested slopes on the right (see Walk 3) and continue ahead to cross the Savica River by a wooden bridge to reach the Koča pri Savici.

Both the Savici hut and the Savica Inn are situated around a large car parking area and each reaps a healthy trade from the many coach tours and day-trippers that come to view the falls. Regular bus services run to Ribčev Laz during high season.

Pass the two inns and continue on a wide track into woods to reach a wooden kiosk selling the usual souvenirs and collecting the entrance fee to the falls. Cross a quaint stone bridge leading over the river from where prepared steps lead up through trees and rock outcrops to reach a small shelter. More steps now lead down to the water's edge and the falls.

The water gushes from holes in the Komarča cliffs and is fed via a series of subterranean streams, caverns and grottoes from the Triglav lakes 1,000m above. The falls are in two parts; the main water spout is 836m above sea level and falls 71m to a large hollow in the rock which has been dammed to maintain the level, and the second fall drops 25m. The complex nature of the underground water system leads to large variations in levels and at times of drought the higher fall may stop altogether. An exploration of the water course at such a time revealed a 100m deep grotto in the cliff containing several small lakes, one of which feeds the smaller fall. A second source from the mountain interior remains as yet undiscovered. A spectacular rainbow is formed over the rock walls above when the sun is on the water in the early morning. The falls are the source of the Savica River which flows into Lake Bohinj in turn feeding the Sava Bohinjka on its long journey east to join the Danube at Begrade before draining to the Black Sea on the eastern shores of Romania. The Sava Bohinjka together with the Sava Dolinka is responsible for draining the eastern half of the Julian Alps.

Descend the steps from the falls to reach a junction with a small path leading off right into forest (signposted Dom na Komni 2¹/₂ hours). Follow the leaf-covered path maintaining a traverse line across two small bouldery sections before climbing steeply to the right to a path junction. Turn left and descend into a large area of boulders. Target waymarks lead from boulder to boulder without losing height to a path that, after an initial ascent on rock, turns left and descends under the cover of beech. At a junction turn left following signs to Koča pri Savici 15 minutes. Continue descending on a beautiful terraced walkway that leads easily through sweeping curves down the forested slope to join the main track leading up from the Savici hut below the souvenir kiosk.

Turn right and descend to the large car parking area and follow the road which leads off to the right. After about 1km, just past a chalet take an obvious track on the left to cross a lightly wooded section before emerging in open meadows at an old barn. Continue directly ahead climbing through sections of woodland to cross a small stream. To the left rises the wooded mound of Ukanška Glava (574m), a glacial moraine left after the retreat of the Bohinj glacier. The path passes through a collection of chalets before joining the main road at the Hotel Zlatorog in Ukanc from where the bus may be caught back to Ribčev Laz.


## WALK 3: UKANC - ČRNO JEZERO (BLACK LAKE) - UKANC

| | |
|---|---|
| *Maps:* | Julian Alps - Bohinj (1:20,000) |
| | Julian Alps - East part (1:50,000), Triglav National Park (1:50,000) |
| *Walking Time:* | 4¹/₂ hours |
| *Grading:* | Difficult. The route is well waymarked throughout and all difficult sections of the ascent are protected or equipped with aid. There is some degree of exposure on sections of route particularly on descent. |
| *Highest Altitude:* | 1,319m |

*Črno Jezero (The Black Lake) in the Lopucniška Dolina Valley above Komarča*

*Lowest Altitude:*     654m
*Approx. Distance:*   10km

A dominant feature of the scenery around Lake Bohinj is the towering cliffline of Komarča. The cliffs mark the southern edge of the Komna mountain plateau, a rugged region of barren peaks and dry valleys that extend north to the slopes of Triglav. The limestone rock is very porous and the mountain interior is riddled with a complex interconnection of underground caves, grottoes, caverns and water courses that drain into the lower valleys. The most pronounced of these features are the seven Triglav Lakes, the only remnants of a once fertile area. This walk follows a route over the seemingly insurmountable rock wall at the head of the Bohinj Valley to reach the remote hanging valley of Lopučniška Dolina and Črno Jezero (Black Lake), one of the seven Triglav Lakes. The walk

81

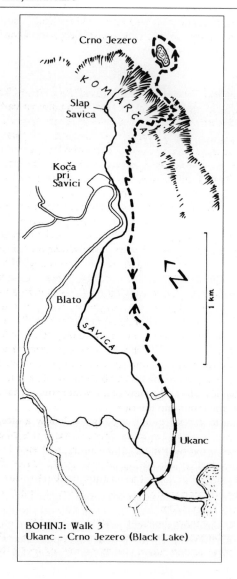

BOHINJ: Walk 3
Ukanc - Crno Jezero (Black Lake)

is an exciting excursion to the Komna plaeau and is suitable for anybody who enjoys simple rock scrambling and is confident in reasonably exposed situations.

## THE WALK

Take the bus from Ribčev Laz to the Hotel Zlatorag at Ukanc. The Komarča cliffs loom ominiously ahead, rising almost vertically to the summit of Orlič at the head of the valley. From this position it is difficult to imagine how any path can safely overcome this fearsome barrier. Cross the Savica stream by a wooden bridge and continue on a good track following signs to Slap Savica. The track gently ascends for about three kilometres through open sections of meadow and into forest to reach a junction where a path leads up a tree covered slope on the right (signposted Črno Jezero $1^3/_4$ hours).

Leave the main track and begin ascending immediately beneath a high canopy of beech on a path that meanders around large boulders, crossing tangles of tree roots that choke the thin veneer of soil. The ascent becomes progressively more rocky with the tree cover gradually thinning until the path emerges at the base of a limestone wall. The barren rock above is decked in a variety of stunted shrubs and grasses that cling precariously to their fragile existence as testament to nature's ingenuity and resilience. Views back to the valley floor reveal only the shining waters of the Savica River winding a course through a dense tree covering. The path re-enters the trees and after a short rock step begins an easy traverse.

A track leading off to the left can be followed to a vantage point above the Savica falls and a view of the water source that feeds the Savica from the mountain interior.

Continue to ascend gentle zig-zags to below a steeper rock section where the route begins to follow a more intricate path. A wire handrail provides security up a sloping rock step to an easier section before further scrambling leads back under tree cover. The nature of the terrain makes it almost impossible to stray from the path, but the route is generously endowed with waymarks including height marks every 100m.

Emerge, once more, beneath a rock face with impressive views across the valley to the peaks of Vogel, Meja and Škrbino on the lower Bohinj mountain ridge. Traverse carefully along the base of the cliff on a sloping shelf of rock to continue on a long rising traverse line punctuated by occasional rock steps and short zig-zags that maintain upward progress.

Negotiate an awkward corner to continue more easily by zig-zags that climb a wooded slope littered with large boulders. At 1,200m wire handrails protect the path as it rounds another corner above a deep ravine. From here iron spikes provide useful holds to continue the ascent over a further section of rock that leads to a fine viewpoint across the Bohinj Valley below. A handrail discourages close inspection of the steep drop to the left of the path! A short ascent leads into a dense forest where a good track continues easily through the cool canopy to emerge at the Lopučniška Dolina Valley by the waters of Črno Jezero.

The lake lies at the base of dusty scree slopes, its shoreline littered with chaotic piles of huge boulders. To the right rise the impressive cliffs of Stador leading to the huge mountain plateau of Fužinarska Visoravan. At the head of the picturesque valley is the Bela Skala ridge, guarding the entrance to the Dolina Triglavskih Jezer (Valley of the Triglav Lakes). Črno Jezero (Black Lake) is the most southerly of the seven Triglav Lakes and is named after the dark appearance of the water imparted by the shade of the surrounding forest. The lake is 150m long, 80m wide and 20m deep and is interconnected with the other Triglav lakes through the porous mountain interior that drains the plateau to the Savica river in the Bohinj Valley below. As a result of these complex interconnections the water level of Črno Jezero may vary by as much as 10m. The barren terrain provides a unique habitat for a variety of flora and fauna including the mountain triton lizard which can only be found on the shores of Črno Jezero.

Descent is by the reverse of the ascent route. Special care is required when descending the rock sections where the feeling of exposure may be more acute. The rock can also be slippery when wet. Sections of the path are also littered with loose rock and debris and care is needed to avoid knocking this down on to other parties on the slope below.

## WALK 4: RIBČEV LAZ - BROD - BOHINJSKA BISTRICA - BISTIRCA SPRINGS (IZVIR BISTRICA) - POLJE - RIBČEV LAZ

| | |
|---|---|
| *Maps:* | Panoramic map of Bohinj, Julian Alps - East part (1:50,000), Triglav National Park (1:50,000) |
| *Walking Time:* | 4 hours |
| *Grading:* | Moderate. Generally easy walking on good waymarked paths. A wooden bridge that crosses the Bistrica stream above the springs demands care and the ascent from the waterfall is steep. |
| *Highest Altitude:* | 700m |
| *Lowest Altitude:* | 525m |
| *Approx. Distance:* | 18km |

This pleasant walk follows the left bank of the Sava Bohinjka along the lower Bohinj Valley to the quaint village of Brod. From here the path climbs over open pasture and meadow to descend into Bohinjska Bistrica. The return route begins in forest to visit the source of the Bistrica River before climbing steeply on the slopes of Čibrovica to reach more rolling pastures that lead to Polje. The road is then followed on the right bank of the Sava Bohinjka back to the starting point at Ribčev Laz.

THE WALK

At the stone bridge by the lake in Ribčev Laz, cross the Sava Bohinjka on the road leading to Stara Fužina (signposted Srednja Vas 4km). Pass the church of St John the Baptist on the right and follow the road beneath an avenue of beech to reach a right turn (signposted Brod - 4). Cross a stream and continue around to the right, past a group of houses, to join a good track that crosses a small pasture before ascending slightly to level pleasantly by the forest fringe. Leave the main track by a path that descends around trees and rock before continuing by the babbling waters of the Sava Bohinjka. Fork right at a junction and cross a small stream to emerge into rolling pastureland with fine views across the valley. Pass a small barn on the left (waymark) and continue through more open

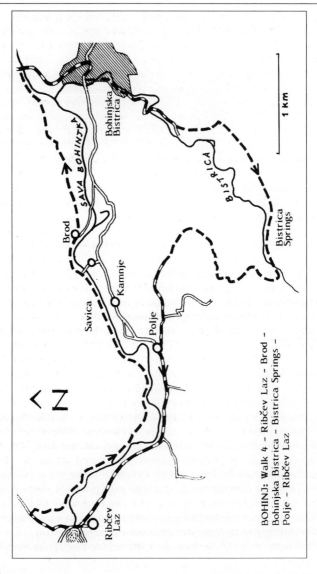

BOHINJ: Walk 4 – Ribčev Laz – Brod – Bohinjska Bistrica – Bistrica Springs – Polje – Ribčev Laz

ground littered with copses of beech before swinging around to the right to follow a hedge line and small stone wall. Continue along a faint path through enchanting glades with the wooded slopes of Rsnik (805m) rising to the left to arrive at a good track. Pass through two wooden gates to rejoin the water's edge beneath an impressive limestone cliff before continuing along an avenue of pine with opening views of the valley ahead. Rejoin the river once more and continue through a pleasant shaded section to enter more open pasture before reaching a road. The wooden bridge that crosses the river on the right leads out through the village of Savica to the main Bled-Bohinj road from where a bus may be caught back to Ribčev Laz.

To continue the walk turn left along the road (signposted Brod), ascending slightly past a collection of pretty chalets and barns to reach the village of Brod at the foot of Rudnica. The old church in the centre of the village has an interesting fresco of St Christopher. At a small religious shrine leave the road on the left to follow a track that leads out into meadows with a magnificent panorama of the valley and surrounding peaks. Continue through small thickets before the track begins to meander down to rejoin the Sava Bohinjka. The river appears to have acquired a greater urgency since the road bridge at Brod, now boiling over a series of rapids. Join a track that descends from the left and continue straight ahead to reach the main Bled-Bohinj road. Ahead can be seen the picturesque village of Bitnje, huddled beneath the rocky slopes of Savica (856m). The prominent church of the assumption of the Virgin stands to the left of a wooded mound that formed the site of a fortified settlement in the eighth to ninth centuries.

Turn right and follow the road across the river and into the town of Bohinjska Bistrica. The town has a very helpful tourist information office and many sites of interest including the impressive church of St Miklavz and two interesting museums. In the centre of the town is a memorial to the fallen soldiers in the last war.

Continue along the main road past the post office from where buses may be caught back to Ribčev Laz, and cross the small Bistrica stream. Turn left opposite a religious shrine and follow the narrow road around right to rejoin the river by a slack pool alive with playful trout. Leave the road as it swings around left to cross the river, for a gravel track that continues directly ahead before it too swings left to cross the river by a bridge. This section of the route is waymarked with the number 8 inside a blue triangle.

The track now leads into forest to emerge at a group of houses known collectively as Pozabljeno. The track turns left and begins ascending once more into forest before levelling with the Bistrica stream below to the right. Another brief ascent touches a motorable track before immediately descending to reach a small clearing. Swing right and begin descending (waymark on tree) on a path that narrows before joining a more pronounced track that begins a gradual descent to the river.

To the left can be seen the waters of the Bistrica springs foaming from within the hollow interior of bedrock to feed into the Bistrica River. Continue along to a balcony track above the river to reach a precarious wooden bridge that provides the only means of crossing the water. Cross this with care (well done John!) to the far bank and follow a path that ascends to a junction at a waymarked boulder. The path that descends to the left leads down to a crystal clear pool fed by an enchanting cascade.

Re-ascend the steep forested slope that becomes more bouldery as it climbs in zig-zags to emerge into open grassland. Continue straight ahead in the direction of two chalets with the wooded mound of Čibrovica clearly visible on the right. Enter a pasture, passing a chalet on the left, and descend to an opening in the bottom right of the field which leads across a small stream bed before joining a motorable track and wonderful viewpoint across the valley to Rsnik and Rudnica and to the high peaks beyond. Follow the track through rolling pastureland to reach a road that leads down into the village of Polje.

Reach the main Bled-Bohinj road where a bus may be caught to Ribčev Laz or turn left and continue along the road on foot to complete the walk as it began by the banks of the Sava Bohinjka.

# WALK 5: RIBČEV LAZ - RUDNICA (946m) - STARA FUŽINA - BOHINJSKA BISTRICA

| | |
|---|---|
| *Maps:* | Panoramic map of Bohinj, Julian Alps - East part (1:50,000), Triglav National Park (1:50,000) |
| *Walking Time:* | 5 hours |
| *Grading:* | Moderate. A well waymarked route with some steep sections. |
| *Highest Altitude:* | 946m |
| *Lowest Altitude:* | 525m |
| *Approx. Distance:* | 14km |

The area around the upper and lower Bohinj Valleys is criss-crossed with a network of well waymarked local paths and many variations are possible. The described route attempts to embrace the unique character of the area as well as visiting some of the finest viewpoints over the Bohinj Valleys and of the mountains of the central Julian massif. The walk begins by climbing through forests of beech and high summer pasture to the summit of Rudnica which lies on the modest mountain ridge dividing the upper and lower Bohinj Valleys. The route then descends into the town of Stara Fužina before traversing beneath the impressive southern cliffs of Studor to reach the village of Studor. From here the walk crosses the open pastures of Senožeta to descend into the town of Bohinjska Bistrica from where a bus may be caught back to the starting point at Ribčev Laz.

THE WALK

Begin on the road leading from Ribčev Laz across the Sava Bohinjka to Stara Fužina. Reach a right turn that crosses a small stream and continue directly ahead to fork left at a crude waymark on a rock. Follow the right edge of a small pasture turning left and immediately right at the far end to join a small path that is followed through thick undergrowth into more open ground. Begin ascending under tree cover, passing viewpoints back across the waters of Lake Bohinj and north to the upper Bohinj Valley, Voje and the Komna plateau and reach a clearing where a track leads left to another stunning view of

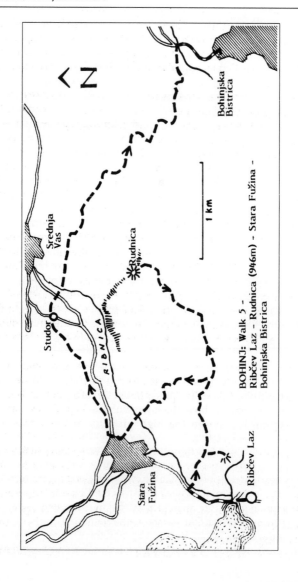

BOHINJ: Walk 5 –
Ribčev Laz – Rudnica (946m) – Stara Fužina –
Bohinjska Bistrica

the lake. The path continues to contour the northern slopes of Peč on an undulating course through sections of pasture and forest, passing derelict barns before finally descending to reach a motorable track. The return trip to the summit of Rudnica from this point takes about $1^{1}/_{2}$ to 2 hours.

Turn right and ascend the track until it is possible to take a small path leading off left. Climb gently at first, passing an old barn on the right, and then more steeply, zig-zagging through sparse tree cover before traversing left on a faint path above a meadow and entering a forest. Follow red waymarks emblazened on tree and boulder trending left and then right to emerge at a beautiful grassy saddle. Ignore a path that crosses the saddle directly ahead but turn left, passing an old barn, before trending right to pick up the continuation path on the far side of the clearing (stone waymark).

Follow the well waymarked path forking right to skirt a beech forest before entering it and finally emerging at the top of a sloping meadow with further stunning views across the lake and to the central massif beyond. Cross further sections of open meadow to pass a modern chalet from where a waymarked rock leads to an opening into a forest at a waymarked tree. Ascend this final steep forest path to reach the summit of Rudnica and views of both the upper and lower Bohinj Valleys. Below can be seen the rolling summer pastures of Senožeta with the wooded mound of Šavnica beyond.

From the summit retrace the route to reach the motorable track and turn right to begin the descent into the upper Bohinj Valley and the town of Stara Fužina. The precipitous cliffs of Studor can be seen rising directly ahead above the town with the Voje Valley carving a course north between the high plateaus of Uskovnica and Fužinarska Visoravan.

Reach the valley floor to cross the River Ribnica and join the road opposite the fifteenth-century gothic church of St Paul in Stara Fužina. Follow signs to Studor-4 that lead behind the church before following a faint path through an iron gate to continue delightfully beneath the shade of apple trees. Join a larger track through a gate with the cliffs of Studor on the left and pass stone walls to enter the pretty village of Studor.

Studor is the smallest settlement in the Bohinj Valley and the livelihood of the people is largely dependent on agriculture. Continue through the collection of picturesque buildings to a religious shrine where a track leaves the road on the left (signposted Brod-4). Cross a small stream with the church of Srednja Vas directly ahead and continue over a surfaced road to an area of cultivated land. Follow signs Brod-4 on a series of tracks criss-crossing farmland to a right turning at a barn that ascends on a faint path through trees to reach the pastures of Senožeta.

Follow over flower carpeted meadows dotted with small barns to the open saddle between the peaks of Rudnica and Šavnica with views back to the upper Bohinj Valley. Turn left on a good track and descend to a junction. The track leading left descends back to the upper Bohinj Valley to arrive at the village of Bohinjska Češnjica from where the road can be followed to Ribčev Laz. A faint path also leads sharp right to the village of Brod but to continue the walk turn right and follow the track around to the right before turning left at a small barn on an indistinct path (no waymark). Climb to a ridge trending left to pass a barn and continue towards a *kozolec* constructed between two pine trees. Pass this and enter the woods behind to cross a stream bed before turning right on a good path that begins the descent into the lower Bohinj Valley. Swing around right with the town of Bohinj Bistrica below on a steepening path to reach the bank of the Sava Bohinjka where a path can be followed right along the north bank of the river to the village of Brod.

Turn left and emerge on the main Bled-Bohinj road which is followed easily across the Sava Bohinjka into Bohinjska Bistrica. Buses run hourly from the post office to Ribčev Laz or Walk 4 may be followed back via the Bistrica springs.

## WALK 6: RIBČEV LAZ - MOSTNICA GORGE - VOJE - RIBČEV LAZ

*Maps:*        Panoramic map of Bohinj, Julian Alps - Bohinj (1:20,000),

Julian Alps - East part (1:50,000), Triglav National Park (1:50,000)

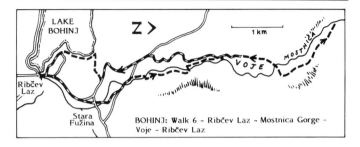

BOHINJ: Walk 6 – Ribčev Laz – Mostnica Gorge – Voje – Ribčev Laz

| | |
|---|---|
| *Walking Time:* | 4 - 4½ hours |
| *Grading:* | Moderate. Generally easy walking with a few steep sections. Well prepared route along the Mostnica gorge with good waymarking throughout. |
| *Highest Altitude:* | 800m |
| *Lowest Altitude:* | 525m |
| *Approx. Distance:* | 15km |

A narrow ravine marks the entrance to the picturesque valley of Voje through which the Mostnica River has sculptured a dramatic course in the porous limestone rock. This walk follows the river along the gorge to the small farming community that still works the flat grassy upper reaches of the cliff lined valley. The path continues to the precipitous valley headwall to the site of the Mostnica falls at the point where the river emerges from within the subterranean water course of the mountain. The walk returns by a track with excellent views across the Bohinj Valley to finish by the shores of Lake Bohinj.

THE WALK
Start at the bridge spanning the Sava Bohinjka and continue along the road to Stara Fužina. Enter the town and take a turning on the left immediately before reaching a bridge crossing the Mostnica River. Follow this narrow road between pretty cottages to cross the river by a second bridge. Turn left on an unsurfaced track to re-cross the river at the Hudičev Most from where the track ascends around

93

*Mostnica falls*

to the right. Leave this track on a path that descends to the right (signposted Voje - 5) and continue pleasantly with the Mostnica River far below on the right. Descend a series of rocky steps to cross a small stream and arrive at a delightful stone bridge that spans the narrow gorge. Cross the ravine and continue on the far bank with the sound of the turbulent waters tempting regular close inspections of the deep channel. Numerous paths lead to the rim of the gorge and although most are secured care is still required when peering down the void. The gorge is 1km long and up to 20m deep.

The path becomes progressively more rocky, ascending a section of polished boulders before continuing along the water's edge. The river bed has been sculptured into a variety of exquisite forms with deep turquoise pools interconnected by shallow runnels overhung by intricate rock amphitheatres that seem to describe the full spectrum of water levels from summer drought to spring spate simultaneously. Numerous sink holes are evidence that the erosive powers of the river are still at work, burrowing to form deep caverns beneath the river bed that will eventually collapse to deepen the channel still further.

The path leaves the water's edge and ascends to a viewpoint into the narrowest section of the gorge. Turn left, cross the river and follow a path right (signposted Voje Slap). The track continuing directly ahead leads back to Stara Fužina. Ascend by steep zig-zags into trees, with regular target waymarking and the sound of the river never too distant, over a section of rougher ground to emerge at a motorable track leading up from Stara Fužina. Turn right and reach the Bohinj. Prvoborcev mountain hut. The hut serves refreshments and the balcony commands a wonderful view over the sun bathed meadows of the upper Voje Valley. Continue along the track beneath the towering cliff walls rising left to the Fužina Visorava plateau towards the head of the valley, beyond which rises the peak of Triglav. To the left of the path numerous springs boil from the perforated bedrock into small pools. Descend on a path flanked by meadows and overhung with beech, sycamore, alder and pine to pass a path junction, following signs to Voje Slap - 5.

Cross the river and continue towards the forested slopes rising to Uskovnica on the far side of the valley. Beyond the Uskovnica plateau is the Shalje Valley where the River Ribnica cuts a similar, although slightly less impressive course to the Mostnica. The path swings around left into open pasture scattered with a charming collection of chalets and barns. The cliffs at the head of the valley present a seemingly impassable barrier but, incredibly, a path does forge a route over the towering rock towards the southern slopes of Triglav. Cross a small stream and pass the last scattering of dwellings to follow a path under the cool canopy of trees that leads up rocky ground to view the river as it emerges from within the mountain in a spectacular 21m cascade.

Retrace the path to the flower choked meadows of the upper valley and continue through this beautiful section with the late afternoon sun warming the flesh and the scent of the meadows filling the senses. Recross the roadbridge and pass the mountain hut, where incidentally the pancakes are rumoured to be excellent, and continue along the track ignoring a sign left to Stara Fužina. Cross the Suha River carving its own intricate course to join the Mostnica above the gorge and join a track descending from the right. As with all the water courses in the area the Suha has its source from within the heart of the surrounding plateaus. The track leads out of tree cover with good views across to the jagged ridge of the lower Bohinj mountains and continues through an area of boulder strewn pastures where the views open out all around. Follow the track until the town of Stara Fužina and the lake can be seen below. The track now swings around a wide loop to the left and descends into the town but take a path leading off to the right (signposted Jezero - 4) that descends through open meadows down to the lake shore. Follow the shoreline around left to a roadhead which leads under a canopy of trees to join the main road opposite the church of St John the Baptist in Ribčev Laz.

*Mojstrovka from the north. Photo: M. & T.Leafe*

## WALK 7: RIBČEV LAZ - HOTEL VOGEL - RIBČEV LAZ

| | |
|---|---|
| *Maps:* | Panoramic map of Bohinj, Julian Alps - Bohinj (1:20,000), |
| | Julian Alps - East part (1:50,000), Triglav National Park (1:50,000) |
| *Walking Time:* | 4 hours (5 - 5$^1$/$_2$ hours in reverse direction). |
| *Grading:* | Easy. An easy forest route with good waymarking. |
| *Highest Altitude:* | 1,535m |
| *Lowest Altitude:* | 525m |
| *Approx. Distance:* | 11$^1$/$_2$km |

This easy walk explores the forested slopes of the lower Bohinj mountains that rise from the southern shore of Lake Bohinj. The route follows a gentle course through forests of beech that provide an undisturbed habitat for a rich variety of plant and animal life. The path begins along an old hunter's track, traversing above the lake shore to reach the Vogel cable car station. The cable car saves a 1,000m climb to the Ski-Hotel Vogel and an excellent balcony view across to the high peaks of the Julian Alps. A path then descends a broad forested ridge back to Ribčev Laz. Enthusiasts may take the route in the reverse direction, which increases the time required for the walk.

## THE WALK

Begin at the stone bridge at the head of Lake Bohinj in Ribčev Laz and follow the road that fringes the lake's southern shore to Ukanc. Pass a small boathouse by the water's edge and take a path leading off left immediately beyond steep cliff equipped for rock climbing on the left. Begin gently ascending into the forest with views across the lake to the right, following signs to Zlatorog - 1. The path crosses a series of small wooden bridges over the numerous streams that drain the upper slopes into Lake Bohinj and begins imperceptively to gain height above the road. Cross a more rocky section and

*Climbing Prisojnik. Photo: G.Sellers*

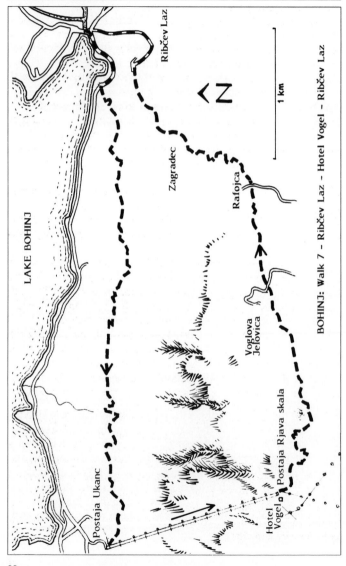

BOHINJ: Walk 7 – Ribčev Laz – Hotel Vogel – Ribčev Laz

another bridge to pass tantalising viewpoints across the lake and reach an open section. Continue once more under the high canopy of beech to cross a stream before ascending slightly as the path begins to meander through the leaves, mosses and ferns that carpet the forest floor. The thick covering of foliage that is so characteristic of the beech forest creates a cool, almost eerie atmosphere lending credibility to every forest fairy tale from childhood.

The path continues over a further series of small bridges, briefly emerging from the trees before swinging left around a huge moss-covered boulder to negotiate a large ravine and a rocky stream bed. Although this section of the route is not waymarked the path is well defined with any areas of uncertainty catered for by occasional signposts.

The character of this route may change considerably as a result of prevailing weather conditions. The many streams that drain the slopes to the valleys are usually dry but in early spring or after a period of heavy rain the bouldery beds can be transformed into foaming torrents.

Continue along a pleasantly undulating course to negotiate a further series of streams until the path widens to a good track. Leave this on the right at a signpost Zlatorog - 1 and follow a smaller path through a series of gentle descents to reach a junction. Turn right and descend easily to the Vogel cable car bottom station.

Cars run every hour on the half hour (more frequently during high season): charges are 52din ascent only, 95din return. The cable car ride itself offers magnificent views over the Bohinj Valley and across to the central Julian massif. The top station is situated adjacent the Ski-Hotel Vogel which serves refreshments and meals and has a cliff top balcony with far reaching views.

The descent route is waymarked (Bellevue. Bohinj. Jezero - 3 hours) and begins by descending left beneath the first chairlift to reach a small path. Ascend this along a route lined with flowers and shrubs to cross a boulder chute before reaching a wide bulldozed track. Follow this briefly before taking a path that leaves on the right and descends through sparse coverings of stunted trees to another track. Descend this before re-entering the forest to traverse a peaceful glade that leads through a covering of beech to a slope carpeted with wild flowers and shrubs.

It is perhaps surprising to find that the beech is dominant over the larch or pine more normally associated with these altitudes. The treeline above Bohinj varies between 1,700 and 1,800m and the local moist, temperate climate is ideally suited to the beech trees. Elsewhere in the Julians, on drier sunnier slopes, the larch and pine will be seen to flourish.

The path continues, with glimpses north across the lake, before descending rocky steps to emerge at the top of a steep slope in a clearing below limestone cliffs. Grasshoppers and crickets thrive amongst the course grasses and shrubs and chirp a shrill welcome to any walker passing through. Reach another clearing with views across the upper and lower Bohinj Valleys and continue on a traverse line past scatterings of beech, larch, sycamore and pine through a carpet of dwarf rhododendron. Enter thicker tree cover and begin descending over rock in a series of zig-zags to pass a waymarked boulder that seems to have provided an unlikely habitat for a multitude of mosses and miniature ferns. Ascend briefly over tangled roots before twisting down steeply to reach an easier balcony section. The tree cover begins to thicken once again before reaching a clearing where the path widens to a track. Cross a motorable track following signs to Bellevue and descend into trees, guided by an excess of waymarks, to fork right from the main track and descend a narrow path over rocky steps. Reach another motorable track which is followed left to a hairpin and a good viewpoint before descending right on a forested ridge. Leave the ridge left at a waymarked tree to continue descending until a track is followed through thinning tree cover to emerge at open pasture ablaze with frolich gentian, yellow gentian, honeysuckle and daisy. Pass a barn and turn right on another track to cross an area of rolling meadow before arriving at the Bellevue Hotel. Continue down the surfaced road to return into Ribčev Laz.

## WALK 8: UKANC - MT VOGEL (1,922m) - UKANC

*Maps:*              Julian Alps - Bohinj (1:20,000),
                      Julian Alps - East part (1:50,000), Triglav National Park (1:50,000)

| | |
|---|---|
| *Walking Time:* | 4 - 4¹/₂ hours |
| *Grading:* | Difficult. The route is well defined and waymarked throughout with sections of exposed ridge that require competence in simple rock scrambling. The range is prone to sudden weather changes and the result of losing the route in fog or cloud would be problematical. Sections of the ridge are exposed to lightning so the walk should be avoided if storms are forecast. |
| *Highest Altitude:* | 1,922m |
| *Lowest Altitude:* | 1,500m |
| *Approx. Distance:* | 10¹/₂km |

The cable-car at Ukanc allows short excursions to be taken above the treeline to the modest peaks of the Lower Bohinj mountain chain. This walk ascends to the ridge before traversing along a good path that climbs to the summit of Vogel (1,922m). The peak offers an outstanding viewpoint over the entire Julian Alps. A fine trip.

It should be noted that due to the friable nature of the rock, paths are under considerable pressure from the effects of erosion. In order to minimise this please keep to the waymarked route at all times.

## THE WALK

Take the bus from Ribčev Laz to Ukanc which stops at the bottom of the road leading left to the Vogel cable-car.

Cars run every hour on the half hour with almost continuous operation during high season: a single ticket is 52din, a return 95din. Take the cablecar to the Ski-Hotel Vogel from where two chair lifts operate to below the ridge at almost 1,800m (32din each chair). The walk is described assuming the use of the first chair only.

Vogel is a rapidly expanding ski centre in a beautiful mountain setting. But stripped of its winter coat of snow the area is a depressing example of man's indifference to the natural landscape. Ski runs have been bulldozed and blasted through the rock and the area is littered with restaurants and dormant ski lifts. Many of the paths marked on the PZS 1:20,000 map covering Bohinj have been obliterated by the bulldozers leaving walkers no choice but to follow wide scar-like tracks of rubble. The extent of future

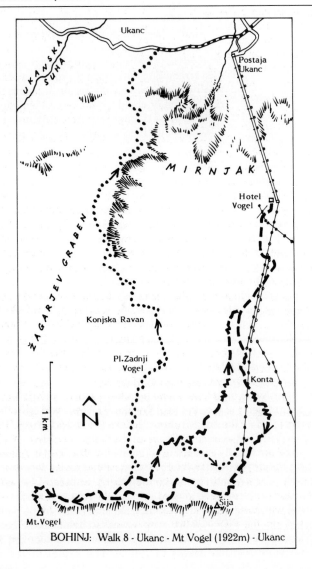

BOHINJ: Walk 8 - Ukanc - Mt Vogel (1922m) - Ukanc

development plans for the area is unclear as is any intention to reinstate the paths. Locals insist that grass and shrub will grow back to cover the tracks and although there is little evidence that this is happening let us hope that they are right.

From the top of the first chairlift ascend directly ahead on a track that trends left to round a corner before descending beneath the second chairlift. Reach an intersection of tracks and follow around right on an undulating course that leads to a final steep slope rising to the terminus of the second chair below the main ridge.

Directly ahead can be seen the summit of Šija (1,880m) and along the ridge to the right rises the pyramid of Vogel. Continue on a small path that leads towards the ridge meandering over rock and around dwarf pine, crossing the incidental summit of Visoki Oriov Rob (1,800m) before descending quite steeply over rock into a depression. Cross this on easy ground before ascending once more over shattered limestone to reach a path traversing below the ridge.

Ignore a faint path that continues to the summit of Šija but turn right and follow the traverse line. The views north over the central Julian massif are magnificent with Triglav clearly dominating the surrounding peaks.

Red dashes waymark the route with the occasional appearance of a red and white target suffixed by the number 1. This indicates that the route forms part of the Slovenian Alpine Traverse Route - a long distance trail that begins at Maribor in the north-east of the country and follows a high level course over the summit of Triglav to finish eventually on the Adriatic coast near Trieste - a journey that would involve over thirty days hard walking.

Continue along a terrace over bouldery ground with the jagged peaks of Meja (1,996m), Vrh Nad Škrbino (2,054m) and Podrta Gora (2,061m) ahead to cross a grassy section before descending to the Vratca col (1,725m) and good views south into the Kneza Valley. Huge amphitheatres of shattered rock fall to the Bohinj Valley on the north side of the ridge and provide an ideal habitat for Chamois which are commonly seen in this area. Continue below the ridge on the north side to reach the rugged cliffs of the east ridge of Vogel. Scramble down over steep rock and follow a faint path that leads to below the north side of the cliffs (follow waymarks for the best route). Continue the traverse, passing a memorial plaque and

*View of Vratca col to Vogel (1922m)*

negotiating a buttress to reach an impressive notch in the main ridge.

Continue climbing, steeply at first and then over easier ground to the main ridge where further scrambling leads to a shingle path. Rejoin the main ridge once more and follow the exposed crest until the path descends across the northern slopes of Vogel to reach a junction. Turn left and begin ascending by zig-zags over shattered rock to gain the crest of the west ridge (follow waymarking carefully) and follow this more easily left with good views on either side. The path continues on the left as the ridge crest becomes more defined finally to scramble up the last few metres over easy rock to reach the summit.

Vogel provides a breathtaking viewpoint over the Bohinj area and beyond to the moutains of the Julians.

Retrace the route of ascent to reach the rocky notch below the east ridge of Vogel and take an obvious path leading steeply down left over boulders to reach a lower path traversing east to west. Turn right and cross another path that descends from the Vratca col and continues to the Zadnji Vogel hut and on to Zlatorog in the valley via the Žagarjev Graben (3½ to 4 hours). Continue traversing, following around left before gently ascending to cross a ridge. Follow an easy path down before ascending once more in zig-zags to the shrub covered mound of Skikaver (1,665m). From here take either the higher path that leads around to join a ski track below the second chairlift that can be followed back to the cable-car, or descend on good zig-zags to join a lower ski track. Cross this and ascend the steep slope directly ahead that swings right to the terminus of the first chairlift. The chairlift may be taken back to the cable-car station; alternatively continue on a track descending to the left before trending right to pass under the chair. The track continues around left to pass beneath the chair once more before ascending around small chalets to reach the cable-car top station.

## WALK 9: RIBČEV LAZ - TRIGLAV (2,864m) - RIBČEV LAZ

| | |
|---|---|
| *Maps:* | PZS Julian Alps (1:20,000) - Bohinj, PZS Julian Alps (1:20,000) - Triglav, |
| | Julian Alps - East part (1:50,000), Julian Alps - West part (1:50,000), Triglav National Park (1:50,000) |
| *Walking Time:* | **Day 1** Ribvčev Laz - Planica Hut 7 hours. |
| | **Day 2** Planica Hut - Koca pri Triglav 9 hours. |
| | **Day 3** Koca pri Triglav - Ribčev Laz 6 hours. |
| *Grading:* | Very Difficult. This grading reflects the seriousness that must be associated with any multiday mountain expedition. The route is well waymarked throughout, the lower section having junctions signposted with times and destinations of all paths. In the high mountains the route is marked using red paint on the rock. All technically difficult sections are protected with artificial aids although sections of the ridges are subject to considerable exposure. Previous |

experience in alpine mountain walking, or British winter hill walking would be a prerequisite and as with any trip into the high mountains the expedition should be thoroughly planned with due regard to the ability of the party, prevailing conditions and weather.

Due to the nature of the brittle limestone rock, routes are littered with loose debris. Care should be exercised at all times to avoid knocking loose material on to other parties who may be lower down the route. This is particularly applicable to the ridge sections on Triglav.

Late lying snow and ice can also increase the technical difficulties. Walkers familiar with the use of ice axe, crampon and rope should consider their use for added security in these conditions.

For parties wishing to make the ascent but unsure of their own abilities, mountain guides can be employed. Enquiries should be made at the Tourist Information Office at Ribčev Laz. Guides may also be booked in advance and more information may be obtained from the Slovenian Alpine Club.

| | |
|---|---|
| *Highest Altitude:* | 2,864m |
| *Lowest Altitude:* | 525m |
| *Approx. Distance:* | 40km |

Triglav is the highest peak in the Julian Alps and the symbol of Slovenia. It forms a majestic centrepiece to the national park that bears its name and an ascent to its summit is an unforgettable experience.

The summit was first reached in August 1778 by a German Surgeon Lorenz Willonitzer, assisted by three Bohinj guides. A statue commemorating the 200th anniversary of the ascent is erected by the lake in Bohinj.

The Slovene people remain passionate about Triglav and it is supposedly part of the national duty of every Slovene to climb the peak at least once during his or her lifetime. Many people make the

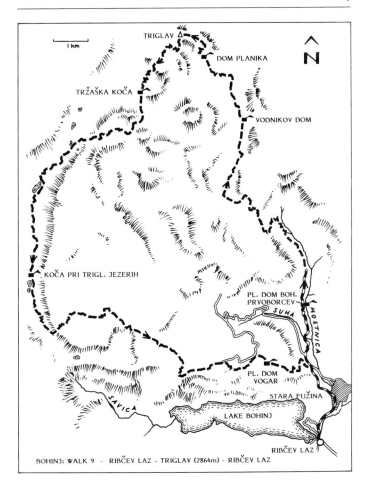

BOHINJ: WALK 9 - RIBČEV LAZ - TRIGLAV (2864m) - RIBČEV LAZ

ascent but the mountain has lost none of its classic dignity for this mass intrusion.

The mountain has three summit ridges, of which all are equipped and provide the popular routes of ascent from the north, south and east. The NE face of the mountain is arguably its most impressive

107

feature, rising steeply above the Vrata Valley in a sweep of snow, ice and terraced rock walls. The southern approaches are more pastoral, but no less impressive for that, giving the mountain its classic profile.

There are many approaches to Triglav. Most parties choose to traverse the peak, selecting a combination of routes that allows as much of the area to be explored in one expedition as possible. Ascents generally involve an overnight stay at either the Triglavski or Planika Huts, both of which are situated to the east of the summit.

The route described here is from the south, starting from the valley base of Bohinj. The ascent involves over twenty hours of walking spread over three days with overnight stops at Planica and Koča pri Triglav jezerih Huts. The route is well waymarked throughout and very popular, which can mean a certain amount of overcrowding at the height of the summer season. The summit ridges present the most difficult section of the route. The ridges are sharp and in some places the exposure quite considerable although any areas of technical difficulty are safeguarded by cables, rungs, metal spikes and steps cut directly into the rock. The route has been described assuming experience of mountain walking over rough alpine terrain. As with any expedition of this nature due regard must always be given to prevailing conditions of weather, temperature, levels of fatigue etc. The mountain should never be underestimated. Late lying snow and ice may increase technical difficulty of the ridge sections and consideration should be given to a rope and ice axe.

## THE WALK

### Day 1

Start at the bridge spanning the Sava Bohinjski in Ribčev Laz and continue along the road to Stara Fužina. Take the first lane leading north to a junction and follow an ascending track left with good views back across the lake, blanketed by the early morning mist. The motorable track crosses an open section of boulder strewn pasture before entering a canopy of trees. Keep right at a fork and continue ascending gently to emerge at the Bohinj Prvoborcev mountain hut after about an hour.

The Voje Valley is a classic glacial formation with steep cliffs rising west to the Fužina Visorava plateau and east to Uskovnica. Continue along the track towards the impressive valley head following signs for Vodnikov Dom. The scarred glacial cliffs that line the valley begin to close in as the track narrows, passing into open pastureland. Ignore a sign that leads across the Mostnica River but continue along the left bank. Just as the valley headwall begins to present a seemingly impassable barrier the path swings left and begins to climb in steep zig-zags beneath a welcome cover of trees. Over 400m of height is gained before the alpine meadows of Grintovica allow glimpses back into the valley. Subtle changes can already begin to be detected in the landscape; the topsoil begins to thin, exposing the familiar limestone rock features that typify the high mountain scenery of the area. The path winds an increasingly unpredictable route in order to negotiate the natural barriers of rock, before the walker is rewarded by a view of Triglav directly ahead. A series of rises doesn't bring the mountain noticeably closer but after a total of 4 to 5 hours walking the Vodnikov Hut (1,815m) is a welcome sight.

The hut is situated at the junction of several paths below the steep west face of Tosc (2,275m) and provides a welcome break from the morning's work. It has accommodation for over fifty people but seems to be used mainly as a refreshment stop.

Follow the path NW climbing steadily while traversing the steep slopes of Vernar (2,225m) and Cinkelman (2,124m). Steeper sections of the path are secured with spikes and cables but eventually the angle eases and a saddle is reached at Konjski Preval (2,020m) where a spectacular panorama unfolds.

The saddle lies at the intersection of a number of paths and care is required in poor visibility. Follow signs left (Planica Dom) and climb in easy zig-zags over scree and rock to below the south side of the east ridge of Triglav to reach the Planica Hut at 2,408m. The hut has a restaurant and places for sixty-five people (7 hours from Ribčev Laz).

The Triglavski Hut can be reached from the saddle in 2 hours and may be a better option if there is any uncertainty about the weather. The hut is the highest in the Julian Alps and has its own meteorological station.

## Day 2

An early start is advisable in order that the summit view can be appreciated with the benefit of the clear morning air.

The path climbs across scree to the east ridge below the SE spur of Mali Triglav (2,725m). The route now remains faithful to the crest of the ridge in a spectacular position. The impressive north side of the mountain heightens the sense of exposure as the path winds delicately along the knife edge towards the summit. The Slovene painter Marko Pernhart and poet Valentin Vodnik are commemorated on two plaques situated between two steep rock steps that mark the last of the technical difficulties to the summit. An artificially created cave can be seen on the south face of the mountain just below the summit. This can provide stranded walkers with emergency shelter.

The view from the summit is extensive with the entire range spread out like a cartographical masterpiece in miniature. The intricacies of the range can be pieced together from this central vantage point with all the major features clearly distinguishable. It is definitely a moment to savour and more than ample reward for the efforts of the past two days.

An unusual feature of the summit is the Aljazev tower, which was brought to the summit in 1895 by Jacob Alijaz, one of the pioneer climbers in the area and can be used by two to three people as shelter. The tower has two memorial plaques: one dedicated to the pioneer climbers of the area and the second to commemorate a postwar ascent of the mountain.

From the summit follow the delicate path that leads along the south ridge, with extensive views across the south face of Triglav, back to the Planica hut. The route has points of aid in many of the steeper sections but these present no real difficulties and the narrow col at 2,659m is quickly reached.

The track continues west over the pass before descending steeply via a series of exposed but secured ledges to the Triglavski podi. The angle begins to ease allowing time to absorb the intricate landscape of sculptured rock formations that characterises the unique high mountain limestone scenery.

A further steepening and a short rise soon brings the Tržaška Hut into view 3 hours after leaving the summit.

The Tržaška Hut, sometimes called the Dolic Hut, provides a welcome break and a chance to appreciate the view back to the domed west face of Triglav with its elongated south ridge reaching out deep into the range.

From the hut the path leads south to the col at Dolič (2,164m) and an important path junction. The path leading SW to Hribarice is steep and slightly intimidating, the bleached rocky terrain offers little relief to the walker beneath a summer's midday sun. Despite this, keep an eye open for the isolated clusters of hardy alpine flowers that still exist, even at this altitude.

The final climb up wide fans of scree brings the saddle at Hribarice. This provides a superb vantage point over the Seven Lakes Valley and across to the peak of Kanjavec (2,568m).

Triglav disappears from view as the path now winds across the Hribarice Plateau with fine views across the brilliant white rock of the Upper Severn Lakes Valley to the Komna mountains beyond. Kanjavec (2,568m) dominates the head of the valley as the path begins a descent into a more fertile landscape.

The waters of the Zeleno jezero (Green Lake) provide a welcome sight, appearing dramatically between the high cliffs at Zelnarica Crag that guard the eastern edge of the valley and the impressive peak of Veliko Spicje. Continue south beneath the imposing cliffs of Kopica (1,685m) and Vel. Tricarica (2,091m), illuminated in the afternoon sun, to pass Veliko jezero (the Great Lake) and in 45mins reach Koča pri Triglav jezerih (1,685m).

The Lakes Hut has a picturesque location between Mocivec and Dvojno jezero (the Double Lake) below the cliffs of Mala Ticarica and provides an idyllic setting at which to rest after a hard day's walking.

## Day 3

A good track leads along the west shore of the double lake and after half an hour a junction is reached. From this point two alternative routes may be followed back to the starting point at Ribčev Laz. The first is to continue south descending steeply into the Lopucniska Valley to reach Črno jezero (the Black Lake), from where route 2 described in this guide can be traced to Ukanc (3½ hours from the Double Lakes Hut). Alternatively the left branch of the path may be taken (signposted Plovcarija and Star Fužina) which climbs above the valley floor to reach the plateau of Fužinarska Visoravan, a region of scattered shepherds' huts and open pasture. Due to its location the area is often neglected by many of the visitors to the park. As a consequence, many rare alpine flowers and animal species thrive in the area. The waymarking is not as intensive as elsewhere on the route and a certain degree of care is required to adhere to the route.

A right turn at Pl. Ovčarija leads into a wonderland of rocky scenery. The terrain is quite forgiving along this section giving the walker time to admire the interesting water sculptured landscape that appears in an infinite variety of shapes and forms.

A short descent brings the colourful summer pasture of Visevnik and a junction of paths. Continue straight ahead on a path that leads across the south slopes of Gor Viševnik (1,723m) and continues across gently undulating upland terrain with views across the Stara Fužina. The path passes the Brezno cave. The entrance is 4m wide and the cave is over 700m deep. The descent continues in earnest through a dense covering of evergreen to reach a clearing by a motorable track. The path enters beneath a high canopy of beech at the far end of the track and continues to reach the edge of the cliff above the north shore of Lake Bohinj. The view extends across the lake to the stony grey silhouette of the lower Bohinj mountains.

The Planica Vogar Hut (1,053m) offers a refreshment stop with outstanding views of Lake Bohinj. The hut is situated in idyllic pastureland 1½ hours from Stara Fužina. Consequently it is very popular with day walkers during the season.

The route continues easily through clusters of farming huts to pass a war memorial before a final steep descent emerges at the roadhead above Stara Fužina.

# KRANJSKA GORA

A summer and winter tourist centre situated on Slovenia's far north-eastern border with Austria and Italy, Kranjska Gora (801m) is a picturesque town and smaller than its international reputation may suggest. Despite this it still manages to meet all the requirements of the modern traveller without losing any of its traditional alpine charm. The town is sited at the junction of the Sava Dolinka and Pišnica Valleys with easy access to the central peaks of the Julian Alps. The nearby valleys of Planica, Vrata, Kot and Krma also provide important starting points for walks and climbs into the mountains and historically, each has played an important role in the region's mountaineering development.

Land quality in the Sava Dolinka Valley has been generally too poor to sustain intensive agricultural development and the history of Kranjska Gora centres around trade which flourished due to its favourable geographical location. Local men who could not find employment at the iron smelteries at Jesenice sought income in the mountains as woodcutters, hunters and later as guides. The established trade routes and proximity of the mountains laid the foundations for the development of the tourist industry.

Kranjska Gora offers the easiest access to the mountains of the four centres described in this guide and also boasts some of the most spectacular mountain scenery in Slovenia. The town has more recently expanded its winter skiing facility to become the largest winter resort in Slovenia.

A good road links Kranjska Gora to the south of the range by the 1,611m pass at Vršič. The pass was built by Russian prisoners during the First World War and provides a convenient starting point for several high mountain walks with regular bus services using the route to link Kranjska Gora with the Trenta Valley and Bovec. Hourly services also run along the Dolinka Valley to Ljubljana. Road access to Kranjska Gora is very good with border crossings at Rateče into Italy and via the Wurzenpass (1,073m) into Austria.

Kranjska Gora has a phenomenal capacity for accommodation

with hotels of all categories, private rooms, motels and apartments which provide a staggering total capacity of 4,000 beds. The town is also well equipped with tourist information, supermarkets, shops, post office, bank, chemist, police station, hospital, garage and vehicle repair centre, and camping facilities are provided at the nearby village of Gozd-Martuljek.

The area has a series of local waymarked walk and the close proximity to the pass at Vršič gives easy access to some of the high mountain routes in the national park. A double chair lift also operates throughout the summer from the town to the Vitranec ridge.

All walks described start at the centre of town by the tourist information office.

## WALK 1: KRANJSKA GORA - VITRANC (1,638m) - CIPRNIK (1,746m) - KRANJSKA GORA

| | |
|---|---|
| *Maps:* | Kranjska Gora z Okolico walking map (1:25,000), Julian Alps - West part (1:50,000), Julian Alps - East part (1:50,000), Triglav National Park (1:50,000) |
| *Walking Time:* | 1$^1$/$_2$ hours |
| *Grading:* | Easy/Moderate. A good path runs along the ridge between the two peaks with only a few short, steep sections. The path has a moderate degree of exposure near the summit of Ciprnik. |
| *Highest Altitude:* | 1,746m |
| *Lowest Altitude:* | 1,555m |
| *Approx. Distance:* | 4$^1$/$_2$km |

To the south-west of Kranjska Gora rises the small forested Vitranec ridge, isolated to the north by the upper Sava Valley, to the west by the Planica Valley and to the south and east by the Mala Pišnica and Pišnica Valleys respectively. The northern slopes of this ridge form the nucleus of Kranjska Goras' skiing development, around which it has built a substantial reputation as a winter resort. The peaks of Vitranc and Ciprnik, while being of only modest altitude, afford fine viewpoints and this short walk provides an excellent opportunity for visitors to orientate themselves with the topography of the surrounding peaks and valleys. Access to the ridge is via the two stage chair lifts that operate throughout the summer from Kranjska Gora. A path links the two summits along the crest of the ridge through a beautiful forest of larch. The only complaint about this walk is that it is too short. Highly recommended.

## THE WALK

Numerous paths lead from the valley to the ridge but a large proportion of these have been swamped by the maze of ski runs that criss-cross the northern slopes. It is therefore easier to make use of the chairlift that gains over 700m of vertical height in two stages from Kranjska Gora. The chair lifts operate from 0900 to 1700 every Wednesday, Friday, Saturday and Sunday throughout the summer. Return fare is very reasonable.

Exit on the right from the top of the second chair and join a path (signposted Ciprnik - 13) to reach the wide crest of the forested ridge. Descend briefly through larch and pine, with glimpses north across the Karavanke mountain range into Austria, to an open area of ground where the path meanders pleasantly to reach a clearing. A steep climb over sections of rock and tangled roots leads to level ground which is followed on the grassy ridge crest through a succession of enchanting forest glades. Descend into a deep

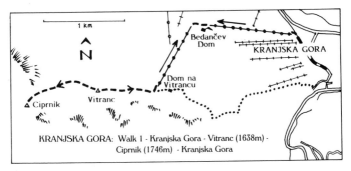

KRANJSKA GORA: Walk 1 - Kranjska Gora - Vitranc (1638m) - Ciprnik (1746m) - Kranjska Gora

*Summit of Ciprnik (1746m)*

depression before climbing again on a widening path that crosses a forested slope to join the wide ridge crest once again. The tree canopy is home to a variety of birds including many woodpeckers that seem undisturbed by the passing walkers. Squirrels and deer are also a common sight in the forest.

Begin climbing an open slope littered with rock and shrub, then traverse over carpets of pine needles to below the rocky western ridge that leads to Ciprnik. Target waymarking appears on tree and rock indicating that the path has been joined by another route which ascends to Ciprnik from the Planica Valley. Climb steadily through a series of zig-zags over numerous easy rock steps before ascending directly through a cover of dwarf pine. The path turns left and continues the ascent with views back across the forested ridge crest to Vitranc. Traverse under slabby rock before crossing it climbing diagonally left to reach a final series of short zig-zags that lead to the grassy summit of Ciprnik.

The panorama from the summit is magnificent. To the west the serrated ridge that forms the boundary with Italy rises steeply from the Planica Valley with the majestic peak of Jalovec at its head. To the south the Sleme plateau is fringed by the mighty cliffs of Mojstrovka with the Robičje ridge descending to Kranjska Gora. The mountain peaks of Prisojnic, Razor and Škrlatica dominate the view to the south-east with Triglav's extensive south-west ridge beyond. To the north, across the Sava Dolinka Valley, the high peaks of Carinthia can be clearly seen over the Karavanke ridge that forms Slovenia's northern border with Austria.

Return is by the same route, stopping perhaps at the Dom Na Vitrancu Hut for refreshments or a snack before descending the chairlift back to Kranjska Gora.

## WALK 2: KRANJSKA GORA - PODKOREN - RATEČE - IZVIR SAVA - KRANJSKA GORA

| | |
|---|---|
| *Maps:* | Kranjska Gora z Okolico walking map (1:25,000), PZS Julian Alps - East part (1:50,000), Julian Alps - West part (1:50,000) Triglav National Park (1:50,000) |
| *Walking Time:* | 3$^{1}/_{2}$ - 4 hours |
| *Grading:* | Easy. Easy walking throughout on good paths, tracks or surfaced roads. |
| *Highest Altitude:* | 925m |
| *Lowest Altitude:* | 810m |
| *Approx. Distance:* | 13$^{1}/_{2}$km |

The walk begins easily through the open pastures of the Sava Dolinka Valley visiting the picturesque alpine villages of Podkoren, and Rateče. The route continues to the Izvir Sava (the source of the mighty Sava River) before returning to Kranjska Gora along the northern slopes of the valley with stunning views across to the peaks of the central Julian massif.

THE WALK
Leave the town centre, following signs to Podkoren - 4, along the Borovska Cesta. Pass the church and turn left to continue along

117

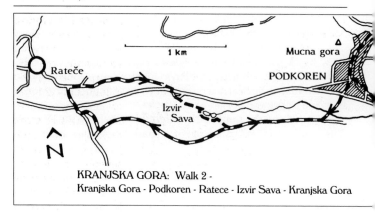

KRANJSKA GORA: Walk 2 -
Kranjska Gora - Podkoren - Ratece - Izvir Sava - Kranjska Gora

Kolotvorfka Vlica to reach a T-junction. Turn right and then left to join a track behind the bus station that leads north beside open fields to the main road. Cross the road and continue over the Sava Dolinka River (signposted Cez Peči - 10, Podkoren - 4) to follow a good track alongside the strange sculptured rock formations of Peči. Take a small path that ascends left into trees (Peči - 10) and climbs easy zig-zags to reach a fine viewpoint on a slab of rock conglomorate.

Continue ascending under tree cover until the path levels and begins a gentle descent that leads around right to a clearing. Turn left through more open woodland along a pleasant path with views across Kranjska Gora to the Velika Pišnica Valley, and emerge into open meadows. A faint path now runs beside a hedge, crossing to a second meadow before reaching a gravel track where signs to Podkoren are followed left and then right and right again at a path junction. Turn left at a second junction to reach a bridge where another right turn leads through trees to a further section of pasture. Continue straight ahead before swinging left on a track that crosses open fields dotted with hay racks and cross the River Suhelj at a ford beside a pretty cottage to join a surfaced road that leads to the main road. Turn right and then left to enter the pretty village of Podkoren.

The village is characteristic of an alpine farming community and has changed little over the past centuries. At the centre stands a magnificent large-leafed lime tree which the ancient Germans

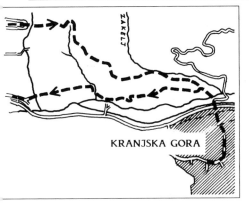

regarded as being sacred. Trees were often planted within settlements and this example betrays the influence of centuries of Germanic rule over the area. The Crna Kuhinja, or Black Kitchen, is a restored seventeenth-century peasant's home in the village where traditional Slovenian meals can be sampled.

Turn left at the village centre and continue down to cross the main road with the peaks of Visoka Ponca, Srednja Ponca and Zadnja Ponca rising defiantly above the trees and meadows of the valley basin ahead. Cross the Sava Dolinka and turn right to continue along a surfaced track lined with open meadow. The dormant ski tows are gradually left behind and the track continues through trees, its grass verges glistening in the early morning sun with dew laden spiders' webs.

As the track nears the entrance to the Planica Valley take a turning on the right about 100m from the road junction and follow it around to join the main road. Across the Planica Valley is the practise ski jumping area where athletes can train for the more prestigious jumping grounds further down the valley. Cross the main road and continue into the village of Rateče. Turn right at a junction by a tree and a small memorial and follow signs to Zelenci - 12. It is worth a small detour into the village to view the church constructed on a prominent mound and surrounded by a fortress like wall.

Continue past old barns and cottages with views across to the Planica Valley and gently descend to reach the road. Cross this, turning left to reach a car park on the right where a small grill bar provides refreshments and snacks. Follow a small path leading into the woods to the right of the grill bar (Zelenci -12) forking left to reach a turquoise lake.

Through the crystal clear water the perforated bed can be seen boiling with the numerous springs that feed from the surrounding hills into this collection pool. From here the waters flow east, swelling with the drainage from the eastern Julians on the long journey to the Black Sea.

Follow the raised walkway around the eastern shore of the lake to join a path on the far side of a stream. Continue past a series of small pools before turning left to join a gravel path that leads through tall reeds to emerge at the corner of a meadow. Cross this behind a hay rack (*Kozolec*) and a small barn on the left to join a surfaced track. Turn left and continue along this walker's motorway bordered by open grassland before forking left at a collection of houses to recross the Sava Dolinka and ascend gently to the main road. Cross this to re-enter the village of Podkoren.

Pass the lime tree at the centre of the village and continue ascending past pretty chalets, barns and one or two larger buildings that suggest a more austere past. Impending attack from over zealous squadrons of domestic geese loitering in the shadows encourages a quickening of pace to reach the Krotnjek River. Ignore an underpass to the right, continuing directly ahead to join the main road on the inside of a hairpin bend from where a magnificent view extends across the valley below. Cross the road and follow a track leading into trees and across a small stream by a picturesque waterfall, before turning right and ascending briefly to continue down between thick forested slopes and patchwork pastures to reach a path junction. Turn sharp right and continue descending under trees to pass a small chalet on the left and emerge in open meadow with outstanding views across the valley to the mountains in the south.

Descend along the meadow edge to a track where a left turn leads across the open fields. Copses of ash, willow and alder line the track that becomes less distinct as it follows a meandering course before entering forest. Follow the track that trends around to the right to cross a wooden bridge before continuing more easily to reach the main road. Reverse the initial stages of the walk to arrive at the centre of Kranjska Gora.

# WALK 3: KRANJSKA GORA - RATEČE - PLANICA DOM
## TAMAR - IZVIR NADIŽE - KRANJSKA GORA

| | |
|---|---|
| *Maps:* | Kranjska Gora z Okolico walking map (1:25,000), Julian Alps - West part (1:50,000) Triglav National Park (1:50,000) |
| *Walking Time:* | $5^{1}/_{2}$ hours |
| *Grading:* | Easy/Moderate. Generally easy walking with moderate gradients. The route along the Planica Valley is waymarked but the return section across the wooded slopes and pastures of Slatne and Kolourati is not. |
| *Highest Altitude:* | 1,200m |
| *Lowest Altitude:* | 810m |
| *Approx. Distance:* | 21km |

The Planica Valley provides the most westerly access to the Slovenian Julians from the Sava Dolinka Valley. The valley is flanked on either side by imposing cliffs that converge at the peak of Jalovec, one of the most picturesque summits in the range. The profile of the mountain as seen from the Planica Valley forms the motif of the Slovenia Alpine Association (PZS).

The walk begins along an easy balcony track that leads from Kranjska Gora into the Planica Valley from where a forest track is followed to the Tamar Mountain Hut at the valley head. Short excursions can be made to view Jalovec and visit the source of the Nadiže River before returning to Kranjska Gora across the forested slopes and pastures of Slatine and Kolourati.

## THE WALK
Follow the main road leading west from the centre of Kranjska Gora. Reach a point where the road turns sharply to the right and continue directly ahead on a surfaced track following the first and last signpost on the route (Planica - 9). Pass the Vritranc chairlift on the left and continue parallel to the main road to reach a section fringed with willow, beech, ash and pine. Pass a collection of houses where the track is joined by a road from Podkoren on the right and

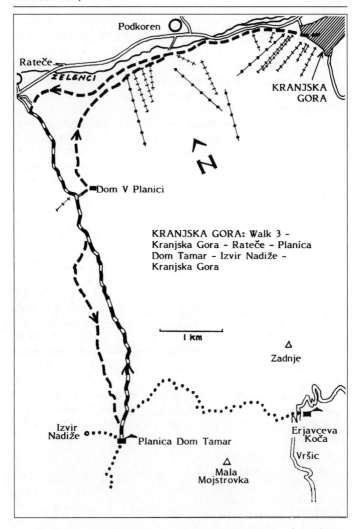

KRANJSKA GORA: Walk 3 -
Kranjska Gora - Rateče - Planica
Dom Tamar - Izvir Nadiže -
Kranjska Gora

continue alongside flowering meadows dotted with *kozolecs* and small barns. The lofty peaks of Visoka, Srednja and Zadnja on the Italian frontier ridge radiate a warm iridescent ochre in the early morning sun and provide a stunning contrast to the cool viridian of the forest fringed pastures. A dense covering of pine temporarily smothers the view before the track emerges at the entrance to the Planica Valley.

Turn left and follow the road into open fields and grandiose scenery. The precipitous cliffwalls that line the valley begin to converge and gradually the verdant plains are overrun by steep slopes of forest and scree. Reach the international ski jumping course taking a moment to contemplate the courage of the athletes that compete here each winter in this suicidal event. The jumps appear formidable enough from the roadside and it is difficult to imagine their seriousness when viewed from the start gate. Planica witnessed the first man ever to jump over 100m in 1936. The longest jumpers today are approaching almost double that!

Continue along the road to pass a large parking area on the left before descending to enter the boundary of the Triglav National Park. Cross an ugly section of gravel workings and as the road begins to ascend take a track forking right into forest along a winter cross-country ski track. The Triglav target waymark begins to appear along the track although the route is not difficult to follow. The track continues on an undulating course through dense coverings of pine and beech broken intermittently by small clearings that offer tantalising glimpses of the surrounding cliffs. Jalovec dominates the view ahead as the track eventually emerges at a wooded car parking area. Turn left to reach the main approach road and follow it right into a beautiful grassy glade and the salubrious Planinsji Dom Tamar.

The Tamar Hut offers a restaurant service and has provision for sleeping up to seventy people. The small Kapela Marije Pomagaj Chapel situated by the hut was constructed in 1936 and from its entrance offers a good view across to the Izvir Nadiže (the source of the Nadiže River). The water foams from a rock fissure situated due west from the chapel, 100m above the valley floor in the cliffs rising to Zadnja Ponca. The stream cascades to the valley floor before being carried in underground channels for the length of the valley to emerge in the spring pools at the source of the Sava Dolinka (Izvir Save) - see Walk 2. A river bed still runs the course of the Planica Valley and carries excess water when the underground streams become flooded during spring thaws or after heavy periods of rain. A path leads to the right of the stream to view the spring (35 minutes return trip from Tamar Hut).

An awesome view of the precipitous headwall of the valley and the peak of Jalovec can be found by continuing past the Tamar Hut on a good path that leads from beneath the cover of trees onto the shrub covered slopes of the úpper valley. The view of Jalovec is tremendous. It is not difficult to understand why the mountain is held in such high regard by the Slovenes. All routes to its prestigious summit are difficult!

The return route descends from the Tamar Hut along the main valley approach road. Pass the car parking area and continue to a path junction. A waymarked route leads off right to the col at Grlo (1,457m) and across the Sleme plateau to the summit of Vratica (1,799m) before descending to the road pass at Vršič (2³/₄ hours). Difficulties are concentrated in the initial ascent to Grlo which involves sections of rock scrambling over moderately exposed ground. The grassy clearing and small lakes on the Sleme plateau are particularly beautiful and the area commands unique views of the surrounding peaks. Bus services run daily from Vršič to Kranjska Gora during high season and weekends only at other times.

Continue along the unsurfaced track to reach a crest before the road descends steeply from where there is a magnificent view back to the head of the valley. Follow the road through sections of gentle descent to reach the ski jumping area and take a road turning right opposite the last jump (signposted Dom Planica). On reaching the hut fork left on a small path and reach an open pasture. Follow around left on the fringe of a forest to join a faint path emerging from the trees on the left. Follow this turning right to cross the open meadow passing a ski tow on the left before entering forest on the far side on a good track. Descend under tree cover to reach the bouldery bed of the Nadiže River where a track ascends to the right and emerges in a beautiful open meadow. Follow a faint path on the

*Sava Dolinka river below Kranjska Gora*

left to pass a splendid large-leafed lime tree and arrive by an old barn. The path descends into trees behind the barn to reach a good forest track with the Nadiže stream bed on the left. Pass an old tree trunk festooned with interesting fungi and emerge from the trees to turn right on a path that ascends into meadow. Follow around left on the lower edge of the meadow to reach a track and continue left to cross further open ground. The track becomes well defined and continues through small copses of pine and beech that fringe the patchwork of rolling meadows. The town of Podkoren can be seen in the valley to the left as the track gently descends, passing under a chairlift before joining a lower track. Continue along this below further ski tows to a large homestead on the right where the route joins a surfaced track. Turn right and follow this easily back to Kranjska Gora.

## WALK 4: KRANJSKA GORA - GALERŠE - SREDNJI VRH - GOZD-MARTULJEK - KRANJSKA GORA

| | |
|---|---|
| *Maps:* | Kranjska Gora z Okolico walking map (1:25,000), Julian Alps - East part (1:50,000) Triglav National Park (1:50,000) |
| *Walking Time:* | 4 hours |

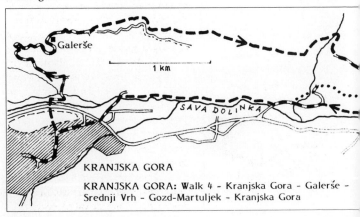

KRANJSKA GORA: Walk 4 - Kranjska Gora - Galerše - Srednji Vrh - Gozd-Martuljek - Kranjska Gora

| | |
|---|---|
| *Grading:* | Easy/Moderate. Easy walking on a signposted route. Waymarking is spurious but generally good. The route has short sections of quite steep ascent but no exposure. |
| *Highest Altitude:* | 1,040m |
| *Lowest Altitude:* | 750m |
| *Approx. Distance:* | 15km |

A magnificent walk that combines the scenery of the high alps with the splendour of the valley pastureland. The route climbs from Kranjska Gora to the hamlet of Galerse from where a sensational balcony path is followed across open meadows with stunning views south to the Velika Pisnica Valley and the high peaks of the central Julians. A spectacular descent from the small farming settlement at Srednji Vrh leads into Gozd-Martuljek from where a pretty path returns to Kranjska Gora along the banks of the Sava Dolinka River.

THE WALK
Follow the Borovska Cesta from the centre of Kranjska Gora to pass the church on the right before turning left into Kolotvorfka Vlica. Turn right at a T-junction to join a track that runs across open fields to the left of the bus station. Pass a series of *kozolecs* to cross the main road and turn right on the far bank of

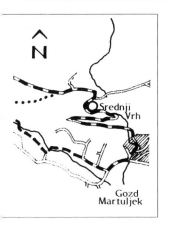

the Sava Dolinka along a track (signposted Galerse). The track swings around left before crossing a small bridge to continue beneath an avenue of horse-chestnut before beginning the steady ascent to Galerse through a series of bends. The path levels briefly to round a hairpin by two pretty cottages before continuing under the shade of pine to reach a metal swing gate.

Pass through this, descending briefly to cross a small stream before emerging in an elevated section of beautiful rolling pastures. This undulating balcony section is quite enchanting with stunning views south over the Sava Dolinka Valley to the mountains beyond. The air is filled with the delicate scent of wild flowers and the hypnotic chiming of cowbells provides a serene accompaniment as the path passes ancient wooden barns to reach a wooden gate.

Continue along a rougher track before descending right at a second gate to join an obvious path that leads left across a small stream. Follow this through bramble and bracken (waymark 2 on large larch tree to the right) and continue the descent through larch and pine, deviating left to avoid a tree that appears to have become a permanent feature of the route, to follow a stream bed before crossing it and continuing on a less defined path to reach a junction. Turn left and begin ascending to reach a steeper, rocky section after which a signpost (Jurež - 10) leads left to continue the ascent through a carpet of wild flowers and ferns. Finally the angle relents and the path descends into the Jureže Graben to cross the River Smec between two small cascades by an insecure wooden plank or, more easily, by stepping stones.

Begin descending pleasantly beneath the shade of beech until a path leads up an unlikely slope on the left (waymark 2). This continues as an easy traverse before emerging at a good track which is followed right to a profusion of signposts that lead delicately through the small farming settlement Jurež. Pass sheepskins and hay drying in the morning sun and descend a motorable track with views down to the valley and the town of Gozd-Martuljek.

At a group of cottages a right turn (signposted Kranjska Gora - 5) may be taken which descends to the banks of the Sava Dolinka in 30 minutes and returns to Kranjska Gora.

Continue straight ahead to descend a track that passes through the quaint hamlet of Srednji Vrh and begins the dramatic descent to the valley. Watch out for a small path leading left from the first hairpin for views into the deep gorge and rapids of the River Jerman. Long sweeping hairpins audaciously negotiate the steep cliffs above Gozd-Martuljek where sections of the unsurfaced road have been literally carved into the rock walls leaving arches and teetering spires along the roadside. Emerge from a short rock tunnel and cross the Jerman River with good views back to the gorge and

the Jermanovi Slapovi waterfalls.

Arrive at the main road and turn right towards Gozd-Martuljek to reach the bridge spanning the Sava Dolinka. The walk may be cut short at this point by continuing into Gozd-Martuljek from where buses run hourly back to Kranjska Gora. To continue the walk turn right before the bridge on a track signposted Hotel Špik and pass a campsite on the right before joining a continuation track into trees. Pass the hotel and tennis courts to reach the river which is crossed on a small wooden bridge to the far bank and turn right (Kranjska Gora - 5) on a faint path that passes a unique design of waterwheel to reach a second, more dynamic bridge. Recross the river for the final time before reaching Kranjska Gora and turn left to continue along the water's edge below scree slopes and cliffs on the right.

The path now meanders away from the river under thicker tree cover to pass a chalet before joining a track that leads to a junction and a bewildering arrangement of signposts. Turn left to cross a stream on a good track lined with a variety of shrubs that leads across a river by a wooden footbridge on the right (Kranjska Gora - 5) and joins a path descending from Srednji Vrh. The route is now more defined and the path continues easily through open glades to cross several streams before beginning to descend once again to the water's edge. Continue through open pastures with the river foaming over a series of rapids to the left to reach the entrance to a meadow where care is required to follow the path sharply left to cross a wooden bridge and continue beside the water's edge to emerge at a road bridge.

Turn left and cross this on a surfaced road that reaches the main valley arterial. On the far side is a car parking area from where a road on the right continues past a supermarket to reach a crossroads adjacent to the main bus station in Kranjska Gora.

*Statue to Julius Kugy, pioneer climber of the Julian Alps, near Trenta.*
*Photo: M. & T.Leafe*

## WALK 5: GOZD-MARTULJEK - SPODNJI SLAP - ZGORNJI SLAP - GOZD-MARTULJEK

| | |
|---|---|
| *Maps:* | Kranjska Gora z Okolico walking map (1:25,000), Julian Alps - East part (1:50,000) Triglav National Park (1:50,000) |
| *Walking Time:* | 4 - 4$^1/_2$ hours |
| *Grading:* | Moderate/Difficult. The path is well waymarked giving generally easy walking with only a small protected section of moderately exposed scrambling that leads to the base of the second waterfall. Two wooden bridges span the gorge in the lower valley and may require a degree of commitment to cross. |
| *Highest Altitude:* | 1,140m |
| *Lowest Altitude:* | 750m |
| *Approx. Distance:* | 8km |

Gozd-Martuljek is situated 3km east of Kranjska Gora on the northern boundary of the Triglav National Park. It is a popular starting point for climbers wishing to explore one of the wildest and, perhaps most beautiful parts of the Julian Alps. The steep-sided valley gives access to the Maruljek group of mountains of which the most prominent is the almost perfect pyramid of Spik. This well prepared route follows through the narrow Martuljek gorge to the 29m lower falls (Spodnji Slap) and continues to the second 120m three level cascade of Zgornji Slap.

### THE WALK
Buses run every hour at twenty past the hour from the main bus station in Kranjska Gora to Ljubljana. The journey to the bus stop opposite the church in Gozd-Martuljek takes about 5 minutes.

From the bus stop continue towards the town to a point where the main road swings around left to cross the Sava Dolinka. A track leads off to the right beside a large panoramic schematic of the valley and surrounding peaks and continues to pass an apartment block on the left. Follow the main track, ignoring a selection of

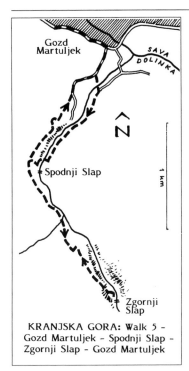

**KRANJSKA GORA: Walk 5 – Gozd Martuljek – Spodnji Slap – Zgornji Slap – Gozd Martuljek**

alternatives leading off left and right, to reach a clearing beside a pretty house on the right.

Leave the main track, which is signposted Privi Slap - 6, and follow a smaller track that leads left (no waymarks). Fork left at a junction to reach the Maruljek flood plain which is crossed on stepping stones or via a temporary footbridge. If, for any reason, the river proves to be impassable, return to the main track and follow signs Privi Slap - 6.

Join a path on the far side of the river and turn right to pass felled timber and enter a pine forest that leads to a wooden bridge by a series of stepped falls at the entrance to the formidable Martuljek gorge. The gorge is 500m long and 100m deep and from this position it is difficult to see how the path will negotiate the narrow channel between the cliffs. Follow a level path (signposted Privi Slap 20 minutes - 6) with the river on the right and continue on a meandering course around the base of the towering gorge walls, descending briefly to the water's edge before climbing to pass a bridge on the right. Continue ascending in zig-zags to reach a second bridge which is crossed to the far side of the gorge and follow a path that leads up a series of wooden steps. Turn right and continue easily to reach a viewing area above the 29m fall of Spodnji Slap that funnels an impressive course through the rock strata.

Continue across another bridge, which at first sight appears to be as precarious as the first, and follow a wooded path across a stream bed to reach a second viewpoint of the fall. Climb a series of steps cut into rock to enter beneath a canopy of tree cover and continue to ascend the slope in combinations of steps and zig-zags. The thundering of the water begins to recede into the distance and the path eventually emerges by a solitary bench and table and a junction. Turn left at a sign announcing an optimistic 30 minutes to the second fall and follow a good track beneath the shade of first beech and then pine to a second junction.

The path ascending to the right leads to a climber's bivouac hut situated beneath the screes descending from the tremendous 950m north face of Spik. The rocky cwm is a world reserved for the alpinist as no walking route ascends to the mountain summit from this direction, but the hut commands an impressive viewpoint of the peak and is worth the detour if time allows.

Follow signs - Slap 11 30 minutes - 6 - and begin to descend with views back to the Martuljek River and beyond to the Sava Dolinka Valley before swinging around left to cross a stream bed. Fork right at a depression to leave the main track at a slightly more realistic sign - 11 Slap 1 hour - and cross a small stream by a wooden bridge before ascending once more, through a beautiful open forest of beech. The route crosses another stream bed before veering away from the Martuljek River and continuing the ascent on a wooded slope to the right. A short traverse provides a temporary respite before the ascent is resumed towards a small rock cliff which is negotiated by a series of zig-zags that climb to the left of a cleft. Climb steadily over rock steps in the base of the depression above guided by occasional target waymarks before leaving it on the right from where the path traverses back left over more rock to reach a junction.

Turn left (11 Slap 10 minutes - 6) and follow a path that traverses over a short steep section to continue more easily below a cliff on the right before descending steeply over rock (wire handrail) to cross a bridge spanning a small stream. Begin ascending awkward zig-zags around a rock buttress on the far bank until the fall comes into view on the right. The water cascades 120m over three falls, the most spectacular of which thunders down a steep corner cleft of imposing rock.

The return route follows the route of ascent to reach the path junction above the first fall from where the track is followed directly ahead. This easy descent route offers good views into the Martuljek gorge and across the Sava Dolinka Valley to the Austrian border beyond. Cross a barrier at a stile and follow the track around right to join another track emerging from the right at an open clearing. Continue straight ahead to leave the National Park where the ascent route is rejoined by the pretty house on the left.

A short walk leads to the main road in Gozd-Martuljek from where a bus may be caught back to Kranjska Gora. An alternative to this would be to follow the footpath along the north bank of the Sava Dolinka from where Kranjska Gora may be reached in under an hour - see description for Walk 4.

## WALK 6: MOJSTRANA - SLAP PERIČNIK - ALJAŽEV DOM - MOJSTRANA

| | |
|---|---|
| *Maps:* | PZS Julian Alps (1:20,000) - Triglav, Julian Alps - East part (1:50,000) Triglav National Park (1:50,000) |
| *Walking Time:* | 3 - 3½ hours |
| *Grading:* | Easy. The walk follows a good waymarked route on track or surfaced road. No route finding difficulties. |
| *Highest Altitude:* | 1,020m |
| *Lowest Altitude:* | 641m |
| *Approx. Distance:* | 12km |

The small town of Mojstrana is now overshadowed as a tourist centre by the more prosperous resort of Kranjska Gora but it still holds a strong strategic position. The Vrata Valley, which leads directly into the heart of the Julian Alps to below the north wall of Triglav, played an important part in the development of alpinism in the area. The view of the towering north wall is no less impressive today and as such the valley road is popular with climbers and walkers alike. The walk follows the course of the Bistrica River up the valley, visiting the impressive twin waterfalls at Peričnik and

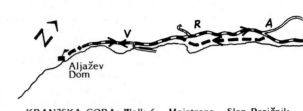

KRANJSKA GORA: Walk 6 - Mojstrana - Slap Peričnik -

continuing to the head of the valley by way of a balcony path to reach the Aljažev mountain hut. Beyond the hut is the famous Spomenik Padlim Partizanom Gornikom memorial which stands in a sensational position below the north face of Triglav.

THE WALK

Kranjska Gora is connected to Mojstrana by hourly buses that run to Ljubljana. Passengers should alight at the stop on the main road above Mojstrana, from where the town can be seen nestling at the head of the Vrata Valley beneath the rocky cliffs of Grančiše (843m). Wooded ridges rise up all around with the rocky peak of Rjavina (2,532m) the only visible reminder of the proximity to the central massif.

Descend into the town crossing the junction of the Bistrica and Dolinka rivers and continue into Mojstrana. The Aljažev Dom is signposted as a right fork at the next junction and this is followed before forking left at another junction to pass a supermarket. Fork right past the Triglav museum (*muzej*) from where the road begins to ascend gently. Pass a somewhat crude relief model of Triglav constructed at the roadside and continue, to enter the boundary of the Triglav National Park. The forest lined road continues through a series of bends to reach a small collection of houses and at the boundary of the National Park central area turn left to cross the Bistrica River via a new iron bridge. On the far bank turn right to reach the junction of three paths. Ignore two tracks that ascend and instead follow a faint path that leads down to the bank of the river. The route continues pleasantly beside the water's edge on a shrub covered flood plain before ascending to the left to join a continuation

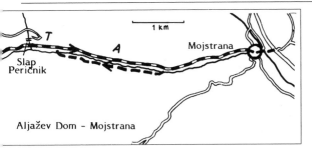

Aljažev Dom - Mojstrana

path that follows around a few metres above the river.

Join a track that crosses the river from the right and follow it left alongside the rushing water. The track meanders through a sparse covering of larch, pine and willow, generally following the course of the river, to lead into series of open glades littered with the tell-tale evidence of illegal camping before reaching a footbridge on the right. Cross this to rejoin the now unsurfaced road and turn left before ascending to reach the Peričnik Inn on the left.

The inn serves refreshments and snacks and is a popular stop for the many coach tours that ferry visitors to the sights in the valley. A sign opposite the inn (Slap Peričnik) leads to a path that climbs a boulder strewn forest slope to arrive below the lower of the two cascades. A wooden bridge crosses the river from where numerous routes lead to the second fall. The easiest of these continues into trees to join a gravel path that zig-zags to the base of a rock cliff. Other routes that scramble over rock to the left of the first fall join the main path at this point. A series of steps ascends through a cleft in the rock (handrail) before traversing right to the base of the second cascade. The water falls 16m from an overhanging rock before dropping a further 29m to the base of the second fall below. A good view of the upper fall can be found by crossing the stream on stepping stones to a point directly beneath the rock gash above. A degree of care is required on the wet rock if tempted by the photographic opportunities, as the cliff edge is not protected.

Descend the steps in the small cliff and continue down the gravel path on good zig-zags to reach the road. Turn right and climb a steep gradient (25%) to continue through a further series of small rises to arrive at a track that leaves the road on the left (signposted

Galerije). Descend into tree cover passing a small chalet on the left with good views across to the cliffs of Črna Gora and reach a clearing and a junction of several paths. Fork right on a rubbly path (waymark on tree on right) that briefly ascends before continuing on a pleasant undulating course. The path narrows with good views down to the Bistrica stream on the left and ahead to the high peaks before continuing beneath an overhanging cliff terrace fringed by cascades of foliage. Follow this delightful balcony section until the path begins to ascend a forested slope over a carpet of leaves and pine needles. Pass a dilapidated barn on the left, its sodden timbers veneered in a collage of mosses, to reach a clearing of hummocked grassland from where the path forks right and continues to climb through thinning tree cover to reach the road.

Turn left and continue to a more open section of boulder strewn pasture and pass the alpine chalets of Turkov Rovt with widening views ahead. Pass a large parking area and continue into an open glade to reach a small chapel and the Aljažev Dom.

The hut is one of the largest in the Julian Alps with the capacity to sleep 180 people. Meals, snacks, souvenirs and light refreshments are also available. The chapel was erected in 1928 to fulfil the dying wish of the local priest.

From the hut continue on a track that leads through a green swing barrier to emerge below the open boulder slopes beneath the towering north wall of Triglav. The vertical height of the cliff is almost 1,500m which gives climbing equal in stature to many in the higher western European ranges. The site is marked by an equally impressive memorial erected in memory of partisans killed during the struggle for independence at the end of the last war. The memorial (Spomenik Padlim Partizanom Gornikom) takes the form of a piton and free-hanging karabiner several metres high.

Regular buses connect Mojstrana to the Aljažev Dom during July/August (check schedules with tourist information office in Kranjska Gora before leaving). However, the walk back is not unpleasant and will take about 2½ hours after which one of the hourly buses from Ljubljana may be taken back to Kranjska Gora.

# WALK 7: KRANJSKA GORA - VRŠIČ (1,611m) - KRANJSKA GORA

| | |
|---|---|
| *Maps:* | Kranjska Gora z Okolico walking map (1:25,000), Julian Alps - East part (1:50,000) Triglav National Park (1:50,000) |
| *Walking Time:* | $3^1/_2$ hours |
| *Grading:* | Moderate. A well waymarked path throughout, the only dangers being from traffic on the road sections. Both the path and road links to Vršič are very popular during weekends. Some moderately steep sections. No exposure. |
| *Highest Altitude:* | 1,611m |
| *Lowest Altitude:* | 810m |
| *Approx. Distance:* | 10km |

The pass at Vršič has always been an important north-south link across the mountains and it remains so today. The road climbs the Velinka Pišnica Valley from Kranjska Gora and ascends through a series of twenty-four hairpins to reach Vršič at 1,611m before descending an equally torturous route to the valley of Trenta and on to Bovec. The road has only recently been surfaced throughout with paved coverings at the bends and carries a good deal of traffic, particularly during the peak summer season. The walk follows a marked path that intersects with the road at various stages during the ascent but climbs mainly through the forested slopes that line the valley. The walk has been described in ascent (so as not to be accused of *always* taking the easy option) with provision for returning to Kranjska Gora by bus. It can, of course, be taken in the reverse direction (2 hours). The route can be combined with either of the two walks described from the pass or in conjunction with a traverse of the Sleme plateau from the Planica Valley (see Walk 3).

## THE WALK

From the centre of Kranjska Gora, follow the road leading south (signposted Vršič 12) passing a collection of cottages and barns with the prominent rock dome of Prisojnik dominating the view ahead.

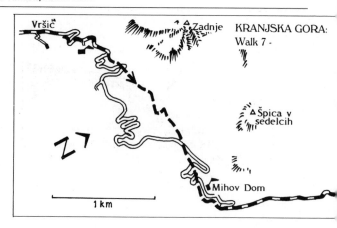

Pass the Hotel Lek on the right and continue along a surfaced path that runs beside the new road under an avenue of horse-chestnut with the Pišnica River meandering sedately in the centre of a huge gravel flood plain to the left.

Take a path that forks right (signposted Vršič - 7) and begin climbing steadily. Pass a barn with views down to the left of the river and the dammed Esna Lake feeding the small hydo-electricity station, and continue pleasantly under tree cover on the western slopes of Mala Vratnik. Cross a junction on a descending path that joins a lower track before emerging on a flood plain at the entrance to the Mala Pišnica Valley. Cross this on a direct line, with good views west to the valley head, the Vitranec ridge and the peak of Ciprnik on the right, to pick up a continuation path on the far side (signposted Erika).

Begin to climb once more on steps of rock and wood to reach a level section beneath small power lines. The path now begins to descend into forest, with glimpses ahead to the peak of Prisojnik, before levelling through a carpet of grass and fern to emerge in the fountained gardens of a large hotel, then to the main road. Turn right and follow the road past Hotel Erika to cross a small stream before continuing on a straight section that leads to the first of a series of hairpin bends. All the bends are numbered and each displays the height above sea level, which provides a rather

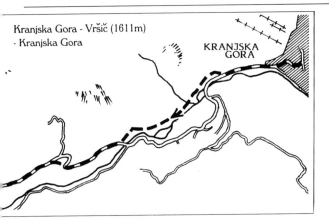

Kranjska Gora - Vršič (1611m)
- Kranjska Gora

KRANJSKA
GORA

unwelcome monitor of upward progress to the pass.

Take a path off left to shortcut the bend and rejoin the road which is followed along a meandering section with modest height gain until the incline begins to steepen as the second hairpin is reached. Pass a crucifix on the right and reach the bend at 1,041m before shortcutting it by a path on the left. Rejoin the road once again and follow it around to the right to pass the Mihov Dom before reaching the next series of bends. This marks the end of the roadwalking section of the route.

A path leads off right to ascend steeply behind the stone wall terrace to cross the road above bend 7, trending right to pick up a continuation path leading steeply from the roadside on the left (target waymark). The path soon eases to reach a junction where a detour can be followed left to view a unique wood latticed Russian church.

The road from Kranjska Gora to Trenta was built by Russian Prisoners during the First World War. The church was constructed in memory of 400 men who died in an avalanche during the winter of 1915/16. The chapel interior is delightfully simple and includes photographs taken after the construction.

Retrace the path into the forest, turning left to continue over a bouldery section to rejoin the road once again. Turn left to cross the road and join a continuation path on the far side (Vršič - 7). Follow this steeply from the road beneath a covering of sycamore, beech and pine to cross a small stream followed by a larger one and continue to ascend another steep section with frequent target waymarking. Cross a wooden footbridge to continue climbing beside a stream before crossing it to enter an open flower strewn glade. The tree cover begins to thin as the path crosses a tongue of scree descending from the Robicje ridge on the right and allows good views left to the north face of Prisojnik with the Okno window clearly visible below the ridge. This rock window forms a major feature of many of the difficult climbing and scrambling routes from this side.

Join the road at 1,418m and shortcut the hairpin to continue along a path that leaves the road at a telegraph pole. Continue into trees, trending left and ascend steeply to reach the road and a splendid view ahead of the razor-like ridge ascending from Vratica pass to the summit of Nad Sitom Glava (2,087m). Follow the road through bouldery pasture lined with larch to shortcut the next bend by a path on the left, with impressive views ahead of the cliffwall of Mala Mojstrovka. To the west the majestic north ridge of Prisojnik falls over the summits of Mala Prsojnik and Golicica into the Suha Pišnica Valley, and beyond the enormous Krnica basin can be seen with its headwall rising to the lofty peaks of Špik, Škrlatica and Razor.

Follow the road over two stone bridges and turn left at a target waymark. Ignore a path that ascends into a tangled covering of dwarf pine on the right and continue on a faint line to the right of a rubble stream bed. The track improves and begins slowly ascending to rejoin the road which is followed easily to Vršič.

To the south side of the pass the Tičarjev Hut is only a few minutes along a track to the left of the road. Further along the same track is the Poštarska Hut. Both offer overnight accommodation, drinks, snacks and souvenirs. Buses run daily back to Kranjska Gora during high season with only a weekend service provided during June and September.

## WALK 8: VRŠIČ - MALA MOJSTOVKA (2,332m) - VRŠIČ

| | |
|---|---|
| *Maps:* | Kranjska Gora z Okolico walking map (1:25,000), PZS Julian Alps (1:20,000) - Triglav, Julian Alps - West part (1:50,000) Triglav National Park (1:50,000) |
| *Walking Time:* | 3 - 3¹/₂ hours |
| *Grading:* | Difficult. The route is well defined until the shattered scree slopes to the south of the summit are reached where the nature of the terrain has encouraged a general free for all. Care is required in descent, particularly in cloud when route finding could cause problems. |
| *Highest Altitude:* | 2,332m |
| *Lowest Altitude:* | 1,611m |
| *Approx. Distance:* | 3¹/₂km |

The height and accessibility of the pass at Vršič makes this a convenient starting point for high mountain excursions in the area. The pass can be reached from either Kranjska Gora or Bovec by public transport and there are ample car parking facilities for walkers with independent transport. Vršič is dominated by two peaks. To the east is the sculptured dome of Prisojnik and to the west the stratified limestone cliffs of Mala Mojstrovka that extend to the peak of Jalovec at the head of the Planica Valley. Each has impressive viewpoints and is a popular trip. The path leaves Vršič and climbs into a large basin surrounded by a seemingly impenetrable barrier of cliffs. A gully leads to the easy angled southern slopes of the peak where the Grenenec ridge is followed to the summit.

KRANJSKA GORA: Walk 8 – Vršič - Mala Mojstrovka (2332m) - Vršič

Due to the nature of the brittle limestone rock, routes into the mountains are invariably littered with a large quantity of rock debris and scree. Care should be exercised at all times to avoid knocking loose material on to other parties that may be lower down the route.

## THE WALK

A path leaves the roadside to the west of Vršič behind a small kiosk opposite the track leading to the Tičarjev and Poštarska mountain huts. The route swings right to pass a waymarked rock (Mojstrovka) and then begins to climb through a covering of larch, beech, dwarf pine, rhododendron and tussocked grass. Pass a path leading to the right and continue climbing in a series of zig-zags, to reach a more bouldery section that meanders across sections of rock before continuing as a long ascending traverse. Follow the path over scree descending from the base of the cliffs heading directly for the large gully that breaches the formidable cliff wall and reach a slightly easier section that crosses grass before continuing over more scree. The position commands good views left across to the peaks of Prisojnik and Razor and down to Vršič.

Reach the base of the cliffs at the far side of the scree and continue ascending around large boulders to enter the wide gully, which turns out to be not nearly as steep as it had looked from lower down the route. Keep close to the base of the cliffs on the right for the easiest route initially before zig-zags lead to the centre of the gully. Scramble the last few metres to emerge on the south side of the cliffs known as Grebenec.

Turn right and follow a path that leads along the edge of the cliff on a meandering course over broken rock. The air is filled with the aromatic scent of dwarf pine as the path continues across short slabby sections of rock. The views begin to open out south to the Trenta and Zadnja Trenta Valleys, with the twin ridges of Ribenzni and Skutnik converging like a wishbone on the pyramid peak of Bavški Grintavec to the south-west.

Join the crest of the ridge at the cliff edge from where the path traverses across the easy angled southern slope over shattered rock slab and scree. The summit can be seen above, marked by a group of large waymarked boulders, and the nature of the terrain has encouraged walkers to find their own route to it. This has, unfortunately, led to numerous paths criss-crossing the slope but waymarks still appear and should be followed to limit the unnecessary erosion of the route.

The traverse line ends at a large waymarked rock from where the path climbs directly to the summit. The worn zig-zags that climb steeply to the summit over loose scree are undoubtedly the most tiring part of the ascent but the view from the top is quite unforgettable and well worth all the effort!

The view north extends well beyond the Sava Dolinka Valley to the snow-capped peaks of Carinthia in Austria. The eastern skyline is pierced by the rocky spires of the central massif and beyond the Planica

*Summit of Velika Mojstrovka (2366m) as seen from Mala Mojstrovka*

Valley to the west the Italian Julians stretch to the horizon.

The slightly higher summit of Velika Mojstrovka (2,366m) rises to the west and, although the route is not waymarked, many people make the 30 minutes return journey which follows the open scree-filled bed of the obvious gully that cuts through the stratified rock cliffs. The route is not difficult and the peak offers an equally extensive viewpoint.

A slightly easier descent from Mala Mojstrovka is to follow the edge of the cliff line east and descend over easy angled slab to regain the path at the ridge crest. This is not recommended in poor visibility due to the proximity of the cliff. Rejoin the path and descend to the open gully where the brave may wish to try the 250m scree run that leads directly down to the roadside. Alternatively retrace the route of ascent traversing the scree to continue down easy zig-zags that lead to the road.

Another short but worthwhile trip is an ascent of the summit of Vršič (1,737m). Situated to the north of both the Tičarjev and Poštaraska Huts this modest summit offers good views of the surrounding area and numerous paths lead easily to the summit from behind either mountain hut.

## WALK 9: VRŠIČ - PRISOJNIK (2,547m) - VRŠIČ

| | |
|---|---|
| *Maps:* | Kranjska Gora z Okolico walking map (1:25,000), PZS Julian Alps (1:20,000) - Triglav, Julian Alps - East part (1:50,000) Triglav National Park (1:50,000) |
| *Walking Time:* | 5$^1/_2$ - 6 hours |
| *Grading:* | Very difficult. This is a serious route that requires experience in mountain scrambling. The path is well waymarked throughout with numerous handrails and iron spikes, but some sections are subject to a considerable degree of exposure. Due regard should be given to the weather forecast before starting as the route would prove dangerous in a storm. Late lying snow and ice in the northern gullies could also cause problems and walkers familiar with the use of ice axe, crampons and rope should consider their use for added security in these conditions. |
| *Highest Altitude:* | 2,547m |
| *Lowest Altitude:* | 1,611m |
| *Approx. Distance:* | 9km |

Prisojnik dominates the view from Kranjska Gora and its proximity to Vršič ensures its popularity, justified by the magnificent views from the summit. There are many routes of varying degrees of difficulty to the peak, but all require a familiarity with mountain scrambling. For walkers confident in moving over rock in exposed situations this route is highly recommended. It is not, however, an excursion on which to learn the skills!

The path follows around the SW ridge, traversing below the south face to join the east ridge which is ascended to the summit. Descent is via the easier south gully which joins the ascent route below the south face at about 1,960m. Difficulty can be reduced to "difficult" standard by using the south gully route in ascent and descent. Once again it should be stressed that care is required to prevent dislodging rocks or other loose material that litters the easy angled rocks on to other parties below.

Vršič is served by daily public transport from both Kranjska Gora and Bovec during July/August with weekend services in June/ September and there are ample car parking facilities for independent

The window on Prisojnik (M & T Leafe)

Jalovec seen from the summit of Prisojnik (M & T Leafe)

travellers. The area can become very crowded on weekends during high season.

## THE WALK

Leave Vršič on a track to the east that leads to the Tičarjev and Poštarska Huts. On reaching the second of the two huts a path continues through dwarf pine and larch (signpost Prisojnik 3 hours). Take this, forking right at the next junction to descend slightly before traversing the southern slopes of Solna Glava over rocky steps. Reach a saddle, from where a well defined track makes a rising traverse across the scree below the east face of the mountain and continue beyond this to climb a series of steep rocky sections. Reach a wooded area from where the path swings around left to climb steeply below a small rock buttress before crossing it (waymark) to reach a grassy saddle. Ignore a path ascending left but continue traversing through dwarf pine, passing a wooden sign (Prisojnik 2 hours) that leads onto open grassy slopes with spectacular views into the Trenta Valley.

The path continues to ascend gently below the south face in

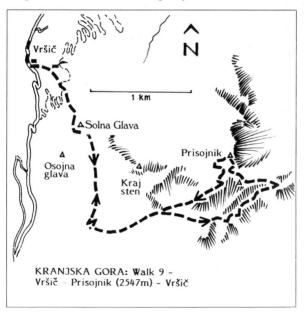

KRANJSKA GORA: Walk 9 –
Vršič – Prisojnik (2547m) – Vršič

spectacular surroundings to pass a path descending to the right (signposted Razor) before reaching another junction. The path ascending to the left climbs the south gully to the summit of Prisojnik and will be the route of descent. It may also be used to ascend the mountain to avoid the difficulties of the east ridge.

Continue ahead across a rocky gully to reach the broken nose of a small buttress. The path passes this, heading towards a large cliff, and begins to ascend left over rock (wire handrail) before traversing right above a gully and arriving at a grassy saddle. Cross this, trending right over large boulders, to ascend a small buttress in a series of zig-zags. Continue around left to reach another buttress which is traversed on a rocky walkway then more easily over grass, shattered rock and shingle. The path follows around an awkward bulging wall (wire handrail) before again climbing more steeply over rock to enter the bed of a shallow gully, which is followed to a notch in the east ridge.

Turn left (waymark Prisojnik) and climb steeply, trending left to gain the ridge from where the route continues briefly on the left (south) of the crest before crossing to the north side and descending a short, steep section (handrail). Climb steeply to the ridge once more to cross an exposed section (handrail) before descending to a ledge that traverses above the northern cliffs with fine views down to Kranjska Gora. Follow the ledge across several exposed sections to reach a steep corner with an open cleft in the rock at its base. The corner is well equipped but the short climb is steep and exposed and forms the crux of the route. Climb this to cross the corner and continue ascending to regain the ridge and the sunshine. Cross to the south of the ridge and continue on a more defined path that follows an ascending traverse over shattered rock slab. At a waymarked boulder climb directly above to reach a wire handrail which leads to a good path. Turn right and follow this through a series of final zig-zags to the summit. Bergheil!

The summit views are stunning. The west is dominated by the peaks of Razor and Triglav, both trailing impressive ridges to the south, forming natural rock barriers between the Trenta and Bohinj Valleys.

Descend initially by the route of ascent but continue along the path above the wire handrail to descend an awkward rock section following waymarks to Okno. Reach an obvious path and turn left (Vrsic) to descend on the crest of a small ridge before leaving it on the right (west) to reach another buttress. Descend this on the right, through a small gap to a gully. A traverse across iron spikes leads to the gully bed which is followed down on a shingle path. As the gully begins to widen the path

*Summit of Prisojnik (2547m) with Razor and Triglav behind*

descends rocks to the right to continue down easy zig-zags in the bed of another gully. The path continues to traverse over rocky steps, following a good shingle track which finally descends in a series of zig-zags over grassy slopes to join the route of ascent. This is then followed easily around the SW ridge and back to Vršič.

An alternative to this difficult walk would be to ascend the summit of Solna Glava (1,748m) to the SW of the Poštarska Hut, which is a fine viewpoint, and continue around the SW ridge of Prisojnik to reach the grassy slopes below the south face, which command a stunning panorama of the Trenta region south of the Julians.

# BOVEC

Bovec (483m) is a small town that lies in the heart of the Bovec basin, an area of wide fertile plains encircled by steep mountain peaks at the confluence of the Soča and Kortnica Valleys. It is the last true alpine settlement in the Soča Valley before the mountains descend steeply to the southern lowlands of Friula. To the north-east the valley enters the National Park and narrows impressively to Trenta, with the trench like tributaries of Možnica, Bavšica and Zadnjica fanning out to penetrate the high peaks of the central Julian massif. Bovec is built below the rocky slopes of Rombon, itself part of the impressive Kanin range that rises to the west of the basin, forming the frontier boundry with Italy.

The area has evidence of early settlement. The fertile soils of the river flood plains are ideal for growing potatoes and other vegetables, while the high pastures provide grazing land for livestock. As in other parts of the region a long established tradition of mining came to an end in the late eighteenth century forcing the Slovenes to return to a more traditional agricultural lifestyle. The intimate knowledge of the mountains gained by generations of herdsmen, woodcutters and shepherds became highly prized by the early climbing pioneers who hired many of these men as guides.

The valley witnessed some of the bitterest fighting of the First World War when over one million soldiers lost their lives along the 80km Soča front. The front line remained unchanged for over two years and as a consequence the area is littered with military cemeteries, memorials, bunkers and trenches as testimony to those dark years. Bovec lost its traditional alpine image after reconstruction of the town following the war, but its interesting combination of modern and traditional building styles with influences from both the Mediterranean and the northern alps adds greatly to its charm and beauty.

Communication links to the region are good, with roads leading into Italy across the pass at Predel and north to Kranjska Gora via Vršič. Regular bus services operate to the Italian border at Nova Gorcia and to the Slovenian capital of Ljubljana.

Bovec has two category B hotels catering for 400 guests, numerous private rooms, a youth hostel and six campsites, the nearest being only 1km from the town centre. Facilities include tourist information, supermarkets, shops, restaurants, post office, police station, hospital, chemist, garage, vehicle repair service and bank. Easy access for walks in the Kanin range is provided by the four-station gondola that climbs to below the summit of Prestreljenik at 2,202m. Bus services run regularly along the Trenta Valley to Kranjska Gora via Vršič which gives access to tours in the high mountains. There is, however, much to keep the walker occupied locally. The area has many natural features of interest in addition to a wealth of cultural and historic monuments. The ever present waters of the Soča River lend the valley a unique pastoral splendour that is a feature of many of the walks described in this guide.

Walks from Bovec are described from the centre of the town by the main bus stop.

## WALK 1: VRŠIČ - IZVIR SOČA - KUGY MONUMENT - MLINARCIA GORGE - ALPINUM JULIANA - NA LOGU

| | |
|---|---|
| *Maps:* | Julian Alps - West part (1:50,000), Triglav National Park (1:50,000) |
| *Walking Time:* | 3 hours |
| *Grading:* | Moderate. The walking is generally easy with few route finding problems. The path from Vršič to the Zadnja Trenta Valley has recently been re-waymarked. The final stage of the route leading to the source of the Soča River involves traversing a steep section of rock with a moderate degree of exposure. The route is well equipped and retreat from the difficult section is possible at any point. |
| | The bridge in the Mlinarcia gorge is suspended on wire and as such is a little on the dynamic side. |
| *Highest Altitude:* | 1,611m |
| *Lowest Altitude:* | 622m |
| *Approx. Distance:* | 12km |

This popular walk provides a pleasant way of viewing the sights of the Upper Trenta region of the Julian Alps. A path descends from the road pass at Vršič through the forested slopes of the Strma Frata and follows the course of the Limarica River to the Zadnja Trenta Valley and the source of the Soča River. The route continues past the Kugy monument to the Korita Valley and the narrow Mlinarcia gorge from where the road is followed to the junction of the Zadnjica and Trenta Valleys and the small hamlet of Na Logu. Buses leave for Vršič each morning (July / August only) and a return bus may be caught at Na Logu. Check bus times at the tourist information centre in Bovec before leaving.

## THE WALK

From Vršič follow the road south to cross a small bridge before short cutting the first bend by a path on the right. Continue along the road to cross a stream before a path (signposted Kizviru Soce Trenta) descends into tree cover on the right. Follow this easily to cross a further series of streams before reaching a motorable track.

Turn right and with good views down to the Zadnja Trenta Valley reach another right turn signposted Soča. Follow this and descend in zig-zags on a shingle path to reach a track which is followed around to the right until a path can be taken left leading into a dense pine forest. Emerge in a more sparsely wooded section and continue through open glades to cross a stream bed, either directly or by way of some precarious logs. Follow the path on the far bank before re-entering trees. A steeper section is taken in zig-zags to reach another log bridge from where the path descends past a huge waymarked boulder and continues down in more zig-zags. Keep left to descend a short rocky section and emerge from the cover of trees to stunning views into the valley below.

Continue the descent on a gently meandering path that swings around right and begins to descend more steeply into the rocky Limarica ravine. Follow the left bank of the river before crossing it by a footbridge and continue on a pretty path to a deserted farming settlement and a surfaced road. Turn right and follow the road to fork right again (Izvir Soča) and reach the Koča Pri Izvir Soča (the hut at the source of the Soča). The hut provides snacks and refreshments and is much favoured by walkers.

A path ascends behind the hut alongside the bouldery Soča stream bed over a series of prepared steps and then by zig-zags to enter a large rock fissure. Traverse around an initial buttress (handrail) and continue along a rock ledge before descending steeply on iron spikes to the bouldery stream bed, at the throat of a gashed corner. Please note that the rock around the stream bed is extremely slippery and care should be taken when scrambling over it.

Fed by an underground lake, the water bursts from the dark fissure dropping 15m to the rocky bed from where the Soča River begins its 136km journey to the Adriatic Sea south of Trieste.

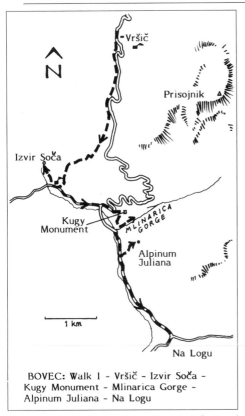

BOVEC: Walk 1 - Vršič - Izvir Soča -
Kugy Monument - Mlinarica Gorge -
Alpinum Juliana - Na Logu

Retrace the route to the surfaced road and turn left to follow it easily out of the Zadnja Trenta Valley and join the main road descending from Vršič. Turn left, ascend to the first hairpin at 824m and take a path leading off to the right. Cross a small footbridge and reach the monument to Dr Julius Kugy.

Julius Kugy (1858-1944) was amongst the first great admirers of the Julian Alps and during his active period of exploration pioneered many new and difficult routes on the peaks of the range. His autobiography *Alpine Pilgrimage* did much to proclaim the virtues of the mountains and the Slovene people. The Slovene Alpine Society returned the tribute by erecting this fine sculpture by Jakob Savinsek.

Continue on a path on the far side of the statue and descend towards a small farmstead. The path swings around left, just before entering the front door of the house, to cross a stile and descend wooden steps into trees. The path widens to reach a small stone wall where a right turn leads down to emerge at a stream. Ascend a series of wooden steps to join a path that once more enters the cover of trees before emerging at the banks of the Soča River. Turn left and follow this past a footbridge and onto a level platform that leads into the gaping gorge ahead. Continue under rock overhangs to a bridge spanning the gorge and descend the steep steps on the far side to view the stream foaming

151

through the narrow fissure in the steep rock wall ahead. A local legend tells of how the devil made this opening by running headlong into the rock whilst attempting to escape from Trenta's parish priest after stealing a holy book from him.

Retrace the path to recross the Soča River by the footbridge and join the main road. Turn left, cross the river once more on the road bridge and continue to reach the Alpinum Juliana (Alpine Botanical Garden) on the left. Ascend on a path that leads through flower strewn rolling meadows to reach the entrance to the garden (small entrance fee).

The garden was founded in 1926 by Albert Bois de Chesne, a friend of Julius Kugy and a keen botanist. Species of flora were collected from all over the Julian Alps and planted in this spot in the Trenta Valley. Paths meander around unique rock gardens and individual species are labelled for easy identification. The garden is quite enchanting and well worth a visit.

Rejoin the road and pass the seventeenth-century church of St Mary on the left and continue down the widening valley. A cemetery of the Russian prisoners of war killed in an avalanche during the construction of the Vršič pass can be viewed on the left. The road reaches the head of the Zanjica Valley at the hamlet of Na Logu where the Zlatorog Hut can provide refreshments while waiting to catch the return bus to Bovec.

## WALK 2: BOVEC - KRŠOVEC GORGE - KAL - KORITNICA - BOVEC

| | |
|---|---|
| *Maps:* | Bovec z Okolico walking map (1:25,000), Julian Alps - West part (1:50,000) Triglav National Park (1:50,000) |
| *Walking Time:* | 3 hours |
| *Grading:* | Easy. The paths are straightforward throughout this walk with only the wire suspension bridge across the Kršovec ravine requiring care in the wet. Local waymarking is scarce although adequate on important sections of the route. |
| *Highest Altitude:* | 500m |
| *Lowest Altitude:* | 390m |
| *Approx. Distance:* | 11$^{1}/_{2}$km |

*The Koritnica valley*

In its brief journey from the source in Zadnja Trenta to the Adriatic Sea the River Soča channels most of the water drainage from the southern side of the Julian Alps. Its water has an iridescent clarity, inspiring many legends and myths that have eclipsed the reality of its sedate meanderings. Only the wide flood plains and the deep cut ravines that line its course betray a more aggressive side to the river's character: a ferocity that is released with the extra burden of water from a spring thaw or a period of heavy rain. One such monument to the power of the Soča is the gorge at Kršovec, where the water has channelled a narrow ravine in the porous limestone rock. This walk crosses the wide Bovec Valley basin to visit the gorge before returning through the villages of Kal and Koritnica to Bovec.

THE WALK
From the town centre head west on the main Tolmin road, turning left at the supermarket to descend a narrow street lined with horse chestnut. Cross the small Gereš stream and turn right into an open field by a religious shrine. Follow the track around to the left passing the airfield on the right with the hummocked ridge running from Log Čezsoški to Krasji Vrh rising in profile directly ahead. The main track swings

153

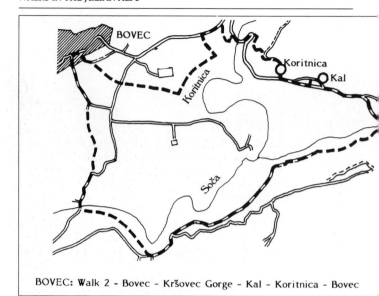

BOVEC: Walk 2 - Bovec - Kršovec Gorge - Kal - Koritnica - Bovec

around to the right, but continue directly ahead on a faint path that becomes more distinct as it enters the cover of trees to arrive at a surfaced road lined with false arcacia, beech and pine. Turn right, following the road down to cross the bridge spanning the Soča River and take a path leading off left to continue along the water's edge before joining a track. Cross the Slatenik River falling from the densely wooded valley on the right and continue straight ahead following signs to Jablenca. The track leads over the Homski Potok stream and continues on a slight incline to pass a right fork, before levelling at the small settlement of Uštinc and good views left across the valley to the rocky peak of Rombon. The track now veers away from the Soča and continues across beautiful open meadows to reach Jablenca. Fork right on the main track that meanders through old cottages and barns and continue along a terrace. A path leads down left at this point to cross the Soča and can be followed back to Bovec (local route waymarks 1).

Continue through open fields interspersed with small orchards and barns, where orange waymarks provide welcome reassurance as the route continues through what appears to be somebody's garden. A

section of grassy hillocks leads to a wooden gate in a stone wall from where a bouldery stream bed is crossed onto a more distinct path that ascends into a canopy of alder. Ignore a path leading down to the water's edge on the left and continue pleasantly through trees until another path (waymarked route 7) descends left to a bridge spanning the Kršovec gorge.

The ravine is 150m long and at its narrowest point only 1.5m wide. The rather dynamic bridge offers a fine view into the deep channel.

Do not cross the bridge but continue along a small path with the gorge on the left to pass a freshwater spring at Zmuklica, cascading from the rocks above to the right. The path ascends slightly to emerge in open pasture after which a collection of cottages is passed before crossing the Soča River to arrive at a surfaced road. Turn left and begin descending beneath the steep slopes rising to Svinjak on the right, to leave the National Park boundary as the valley begins to open out and arrive at the collective settlement of Kal - Koritnica. An unsurfaced track leaves the main road on the right and ascends to the village of Kal. The settlement was at the position of the front line during the First World War and as a consequence suffered terrible damage. Miraculously the small Gothic church that stands in the centre of the village survived the terrible onslaught.

Turn left to rejoin the main road at the site of a monument built in memory of forty-two partisans killed in the Second World War by Italian troops on the Golobar pastures. The memorials that litter the valley are sobering reminders of the suffering of the two world wars.

Continue along the road until it is joined by a track descending from the right and turn right to enter the streets of Koritnica. Weave through the tightly packed cottages and barns bedecked in flowers to reach a water trough on the right from where a road is followed around to the left. Ascend this to reach a sharp right hand bend where a path descends to the left and leads alongside stone walls and pastures. Follow this through a slightly overgrown section to join a path descending from the right which leads down to a surfaced road. Turn right and cross the Koritnica River at the head of the narrow Koritnica Valley with good views to the Krnice ridge ahead.

155

One hundred metres beyond the bridge join a path on the left that ascends into forest (waymark 5a) and rejoins the main road with fine views across the Soča Valley. Continue towards Bovec to pass a large ash tree before taking a track that leads left by a seat and follows alongside open fields. Turn right at the end of a hedgerow to pass a small cottage before joining a larger track on the far side of a ski tow which is followed right, aiming for the small Gothic church on the outskirts of Bovec.

The sixteenth-century church of the Virgin Mary suffered considerable damage during the First World War but still contains late Gothic frescoes that have been preserved.

Cross the surfaced road and continue alongside the church, descending to cross the Geles stream before reaching the hotel Kanin. A narrow side street leads from the hotel to the centre of Bovec.

## WALK 3: BOVEC - GAPEC - IZVIR GLIJUNA - PLUŽNA - VISNA - BOVEC

| | |
|---|---|
| *Maps:* | Bovec z Okolico walking map (1:25,000), |
| | Julian Alps - West part (1:50,000), Triglav National Park (1:50,000) |
| *Walking Time:* | $2^{1}/_{2}$ - 3 hours |
| *Grading:* | Easy. The path is well defined throughout with an excess of waymarking. No exposure or difficulties of any kind. |
| *Highest Altitude:* | 700m |
| *Lowest Altitude:* | 370m |
| *Approx. Distance:* | 9km |

This enjoyable walk climbs through forest and pasture to the confluence of the Glijan and Ročica streams before continuing on to the source of the Glitjuna. The path passes through the charming hamlet of Plužna and the revived sheep pastures in Krinica before descending from the marvellous viewpoint at Visna through forests of beech back to Bovec.

### THE WALK
From the centre of town follow the main road that leads east to Tomlin and wind through the pretty suburbs of Brdo to the hamlet of Dvor.

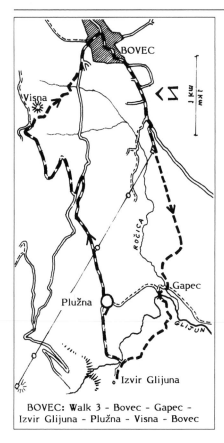

BOVEC: Walk 3 - Bovec - Gapec -
Izvir Glijuna - Plužna - Visna - Bovec

Take a fork on the right opposite a petrol station to the bottom station of the Kanin gondola. Pass this and continue directly ahead on a good track (signposted Plužna) alongside open meadows with views right to the impressive Kanin mountain range. Enter a wood and fork left, guided by a proliferation of orange stripes and circle waymarks, and begin descending before forking right to continue along a beautiful forest path lined with a profusion of exotic flowers, and shrubs.

Reach a junction and turn left (signposted Podklopca and Plužna) following the Ročica stream on the right and join a motorable track. Turn right to cross the river and then sharp left (Jezero) where a small path crosses a stream by an enchanting stone bridge, before skirting around the settlement of Gapec to continue under a shady grove of beech. Begin to ascend before finally emerging at a level concrete pipeduct. Turn right and continue easily along this convenient walkway to arrive at a small man-made reservoir.

The lake is supplied from the River Glijuna and in turn feeds water to the small hydro-electric power station by the roadside at Podklopa. Despite the artificial nature of the reservoir the turquoise waters are delightfully scenic against the mountain backdrop across the valley.

Ignore a path leading left into trees but follow around the eastern

*View from the reservoir at Plužna across the Soča valley*

edge of the lake to reach a quaint chalet. Turn left and continue along the concrete ducts (signpost Izvir Glijuna) to cross between the sparkling pools of a tributary stream before reaching a series of sluces and weirs. Follow a small path that continues over bouldery steps by the river's edge to where the waters of the Glijuna emerge from the mountain interior through a chaotic pile of moss covered boulders.

Retrace the route to a path that leads left and descends to a motorable track. Follow this left across the river by a wooden bridge before ascending to reach a beautifully secluded cottage on the left. The track arrives into open pasture from where a path is followed on the right to cross open grassland with good views across the Bovec basin, and enter the village of Plužna. Follow through the narrow streets, turning right at a memorial to pass the sixteenth-century church on the left before reaching a more open section with further views down to the valley basin. Ignore a path that leaves the track on the right (signposted Bovec) but continue directly ahead to pass under the Kanin gondola before climbing steadily past a number of homesteads to reach a road junction.

Turn left (signposted Kanin, route 3 waymarking) and continue ascending to a chalet where a right fork is taken to Visna. Continue climbing to a hairpin where a path can be taken on the right to Bovec (target waymarking). Ignore this, with the assurance that the views from Visna will be worth all the effort, and climb to another bend where the track begins to level. Pass a path leading left by a water trough to the peak of Rombon and continue around on the lower of two tracks. Take a right fork and almost immediately join a path on the left (signposted Bovec) to descend past a barn and a wooden gate. Continue between two stone walls that fringe grazing land to reach Visna and a magnificent viewpoint to the upper reaches of Trenta and the high peaks of the central Julian Alps.

Descend a quaint stepped path across open meadows and pass through a gate to enter a forest of beech. Continue down this beautiful section, swinging around left to cross the babbling Ubivnica brook to reach another wooden gate. With the modern flats of Kaninska Vas on the right join a surfaced road which leads down to the church of St Urh in Bovec.

The church, sited on a prominent area of high ground with its monumental staircase climbing beneath the external neo-Roman façade, lends the town a sense of grandeur. Inside the decor betrays its Gothic origins and includes a magnificent altar carved from rock.

From the church descend the main road to reach the town centre.

## WALK 4: BOVEC - PLAJER - KLUŽE - BOVEC

| | |
|---|---|
| *Maps:* | Bovec z Okolico walking map (1:25,000), Julian Alps - West part (1:50,000), Triglav National Park (1:50,000) |
| *Walking Time:* | 3$^1$/$_2$ hours |
| *Grading:* | Moderate. The walking is generally easy on well waymarked paths although the ascent to Plajer and descent to Kluže are steep in parts. The route passes through a 200m tunnel for which a small torch may be useful. The suspension bridge that crosses the Koritnica River requires care. |
| *Highest Altitude:* | 900m |
| *Lowest Altitude:* | 460m |
| *Approx. Distance:* | 13km |

This is undoubtedly one of the most beautiful walks in the valley. The ascent to the boulder strewn slopes of Plajer has a distinctly Mediterranean atmosphere and is a good example of the influence the southern climate has on the terrain. The wooded slopes above Kluže however are distinctly Slovene. The path passes the remains of heavy

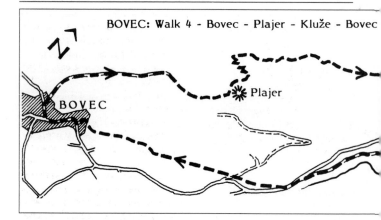

BOVEC: Walk 4 - Bovec - Plajer - Kluže - Bovec

fortifications on the cliffs below Na robu and descends to the fort at Kluže that stands over the impressive Koritnica gorge. The return route to Bovec crosses the Sumnik River and continues through meadows, pastures and forest that typify the natural splendours of the valley.

## THE WALK

From the town centre take the road leading up to the church of St Urh and continue around to the right to pass a sports ground. The road becomes unsurfaced and ascends through a small grove of beech to reach a clearing before swinging right to pass a blockhouse displaying the first of the route waymarks (an orange circle supplemented by the number 4). Pass this to reach a farmstead on a levelling path that crosses a stream, then continues beneath the shade of false acacia, sycamore and beech through open glades of fern and tussocked grass bordered by stone walls. Pass a barn on the right with an unconvincing skull and cross-bones on the door and continue through two wooden gates to reach a small chalet nestled beneath the rocky slopes of Rombon.

Follow the lower of two tracks that traverses a bouldery pasture before continuing along a pleasant grass path that leads into trees. Reach a path junction by a barn and follow route 4, forking left, passing the barn and ascending to an open grassy section before turning left to join a track. Follow the track around a bend and continue straight ahead through a covering of pine to reach a wooden gate that leads into the rugged pasture of Panjer with wonderful views ahead to the Koritnica

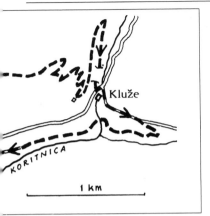

and Soča Valleys.

Pass a barn on the left, built precariously beneath a massif limestone boulder, on a path that leads to a stone wall (waymarked route 5b, Kluže). Follow the wall until the path turns left at a waymarked boulder and begins to ascend the rock littered slope. The path is indistinct at first with many false trails, but the section has a generous number of waymarks that weave a route around the boulders in a series of wide swinging zig-zags. The heavy aromatic air sings with the screeching of grasshoppers and crickets, and common lizards scurry for shelter from the passing walker, giving this section a character normally associated with a more southern latitude.

The route gradually becomes more uniform, ascending into a thickening cover of trees to reach a tongue of scree. Cross this on the right from where a pleasantly undulating path continues more easily beneath a cool canopy of beech.

The hard work is largely behind us now and the path continues on its traverse line through forest punctuated with open grassy slopes, rocky scree and bouldery ravines each offering a different perspective on the views to the valley head and the high peaks beyond. The route gradually begins to descend below a rock buttress to join a path descending from the left. Turn right and continue down the steep wooded slope along a series of countless zig-zags that vary in pitch and length, meandering around buttresses of rock, trees and other obstacles to lose 250m of hard earned height before emerging at the upper fortification of Kluže.

The broken concrete is cloaked with an eerie silence, its walls defenceless against the invasion of undergrowth. The building suffered substantial damage at the hands of the Italian batteries during the First World War and it is difficult to imagine the horrors witnessed by its now silent corridors.

Follow the path back into the forest to join a large balcony below a cliff. This was once the supply route to the upper fortification and is

*Svinjak from the Plajer pastures*

lined with additional strongholds tunnelled into the cliff face. Ignore paths descending to the right, but continue below the cliff to enter forest where the path swings around right to descend in short zig-zags beside a bouldery gully. Continue traversing right to arrive at the entrance to the tunnel where waymarks beckon in the dark interior. Although the exit can be seen from the entrance a torch may be useful as the ground is uneven and often waterlogged.

Emerge with exciting views left into the Koritnica gorge and reach the road opposite the main fortifications at Kluže.

The position above the gorge at the entrance to the Koritnica and Bavšica Valleys has been of strategic importance since the fifteenth century. The fort was constructed in the early seventeenth century and a nearby spring enabled the occupants to endure long sieges. The present appearance of the fort is a result of rebuilding in the late nineteenth century.

Turn left and cross the 80m deep Koritnica gorge. The channel is 500m long and the complex nature of the river course and the narrow overhanging rock walls render it impassable. Turn right (signposted Bavšica) and begin ascending into the Bavšica Valley with glorious views ahead. Leave the road by a track on the right that follows along an old stone wall beneath the shade of trees, before swinging around to the right to reach a second bend where a path leads across an open pasture beside a hedge and into trees. Continue along a rocky terrace with views down to the Koritnica River before descending on zig-zags to reach the water's edge. Follow around to the right on rock ledges to cross the river at a wire suspension bridge with views right of the foaming waters emerging from the gorge. Turn left on a path beneath an old stone ruin and join a track descending from the right. Pass another path that descends left to the river and continue directly ahead into trees with the sound of the turbulent waters on the left.

Emerge at a clearing by a collection of private garages and continue along the good track (signposted Bovec) to arrive eventually at a main road. Follow this left for about 100m then take a path on the right that climbs on the fringe of forest above the road. Cross a motorable track and continue into open pasture, passing isolated barns, cottages and hay racks to reach the settlement of Mala Vas. The track leads between a collection of old and new cottages until it is possible to make a turning left to cross the channelled Geleš stream and arrive at the main road. Turn right and follow this easily into Bovec.

## WALK 5: BOVEC - SLAP BOKA - DOLENJA VAS - ČEZSOČA - BOVEC

| | |
|---|---|
| *Maps:* | Bovec z Okolico walking map (1:25,000), Julian Alps - West part (1:50,000), Triglav National Park (1:50,000) |
| *Walking Time:* | 4¹/₂ - 5 hours |
| *Grading:* | Difficult. The walk to view the falls has no difficulties, following either roads or a well defined track, but the route to the head of the falls climbs over ground which, although secured by numerous handrails, is steep and induces a mild degree of exposure. |
| *Highest Altitude:* | 850m |
| *Lowest Altitude:* | 350m |
| *Approx. Distance:* | 15¹/₂km |

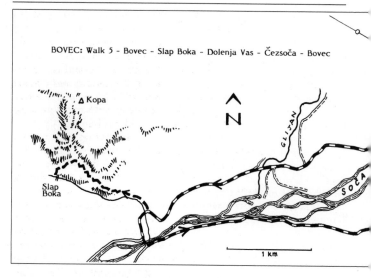

BOVEC: Walk 5 - Bovec - Slap Boka - Dolenja Vas - Čezsoča - Bovec

This walk descends into the widening Soča Valley below Bovec to view the magnificent Boka fall, channelling water from the upper Kanin mountains into one thundering cascade. Two marked paths ascend to the fall; the first ascends to the west to reach a good viewpoint below the fall ($1^{1}/4$ hour return trip from the road), but it is the eastern track that this walk follows, ascending above the head of the fall to the river source. The return route crosses the Soča River to visit the charming villages of Dolenja Vas and Čezsoča before continuing on to Bovec.

## THE WALK
Leave Bovec on the main Tolmin road, passing through the jumbled suburbs of the town to reach a petrol station opposite the turning to the Kanin Gondola. Continue along the main road, descending into the widening Soča Valley to cross the Geles stream before ascending slightly to reach a well tended Second World War memorial on the left. The road now descends through a steep sided channel before views once more open out across the fertile valley basin and the rocky mountain peaks. Reach the hamlet of Podklopca and continue to cross the Glijan River with extensive views above the northern forested slopes of the Kanin range to Kaninski Podi - the unique alpine karst flats

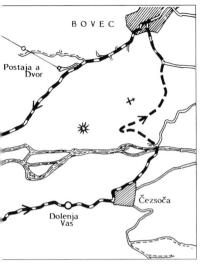

that are such a feature of the high mountain terrain in the region. The road passes through open pastures before reaching the Žvikar Inn and continues across the Sušec stream to swing around to the right and arrive at a new road bridge spanning a bouldery river bed.

Leave the road for a path on the right that follows the bank of the Boka River along the forest fringe to reach a small hut. The path now begins to ascend, crossing a slope of scree before climbing steeply to a rocky buttress. Follow this on or near the crest before continuing in a series of steep zig-zags and gentle rising traverses under the cover of bushy hornbeams. Cross a scree slope and reach a junction where a short detour leads left to a viewpoint into the ravine and across the Soča Valley. The path now climbs a series of rocky ledges cascading with a profusion of wild flowers to traverse a bouldery chute before re-entering tree cover. After a long section of steep zig-zags the angle begins to relent over rock to reach a grassy shoulder. From here it continues climbing in what initially appears to be the wrong direction before a long traverse across a steep wooded slope leads back to the thundering of the falls. Cross a gully and ascend a short rock step (handrail) before descending steeply on the far side of a shoulder in a series of zig-zags (numerous handrails). Traverse beneath an overhanging buttress from where the path leads more easily to the water's edge.

The situation is quite unique with the water roaring over the edge of the cliff on the left, falling well over 100m to the valley floor, and on the right foaming from the mountain interior at the base of a towering cliff.

The route of ascent is reversed to reach the road which is followed across the bridge to a good view of the falls. Continue past a small snack bar and reach a parking area beside the road bridge spanning the Soča.

165

*Cottages in the back streets of Bovec*

The initial roadwalk from Bovec can be avoided by taking one of the regular bus services that run down the valley to this point (deduct 1 hour's walking time).

Cross the River Soča and turn left on the far bank to follow a track that runs beneath the steep wooded slopes of Na Požarju with final views across to the Boka fall and the deep cut ravine below the summit of Kopa. The track leaves the river bank and crosses the open plains of the Bovec basin with the elegant peak of Svinjak dominating the skyline ahead. Continue through the village of Dolenja Vas, where vine and geranium adorn the rickety upper terraces of old cottages and barns, and reach the next settlement at Čezsoča.

Far from being neglected these old communities appear to be prospering with the increasing demand for holiday homes and tourist accommodation. Thankfully, modern chalets are being built in a traditional style that harmonizes with the existing buildings The village of Čezsoča has a beautiful church and also boasts a modest ski facility.

Pass a war memorial on the left, continue to a junction and turn left by an inn before swinging around to the right to reach Gorenja Vas. Pass another inn on the right, serving refreshments and snacks, and arrive at the Soča River. Cross this and ascend a track on the left (signposted Bovec) to climb gently through trees before emerging into open grassland with good views across to Bovec. Ignore a track leading straight across the airfield but turn right on a path that heads for the cover of trees. Emerge to follow the perimeter of the airfield on the left before turning left to join a surfaced road by a small shrine on the right. Follow this along an avenue of horse chestnut to cross the Gereš stream before arriving at the town centre in Bovec.

## WALK 6: BOVEC - KORITNICA - SVINJAK (1,653m) - BOVEC

| | |
|---|---|
| *Maps:* | Bovec z Okolico walking map (1:25,000), Julian Alps - West part (1:50,000), Triglav National Park (1:50,000) |
| *Walking Time:* | 5<sup>1</sup>/2 hours |
| *Grading:* | Difficult. The path follows a well waymarked route and although the ascent is a little demanding there are no route finding difficulties. The path is steep below the summit with a few short sections of easy scrambling. Care is required in descent where the rock is loose in places and the exposure is at its keenest. The suspension bridge crossing the Koritnica at Vodenca was in a bad state of repair in 1990 with many missing or broken boards and represented the boldest section of the entire route. |
| *Highest Altitude:* | 1,653m |
| *Lowest Altitude:* | 400m |
| *Approx. Distance:* | 13<sup>1</sup>/2km |

Between the valleys of Koritnica and Soča rises the pinnacled SW ridge of Bavški Grintavec. Viewed from Bovec the ridge appears as a single peak of such distinctive shape that it has been dubbed "The Matterhorn of Bovec". A marked path ascends the wide ridge crest above the tree line to the rocky prow of Svinjak at 1,653m where the panorama from the summit is unsurpassed.

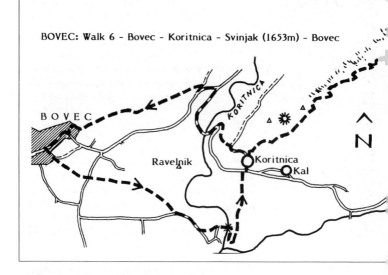

BOVEC: Walk 6 - Bovec - Koritnica - Svinjak (1653m) - Bovec

## THE WALK

From the town centre head west on the main Tolmin Road, turning left at the supermarket to descend a short distance on a narrow street before turning left again into the Kanin Hotel. On the far side of the hotel turn right on a path to cross open fields with the wooded mound of Javoršček rising directly ahead. The path can also be reached by a small alley that leads from the town centre opposite the main road descending from the church.

Cross the Geleš stream and reach the church of the Virgin Mary by the campsite at a surfaced road and continue across this to join a track that follows over a further section of pasture (signposted Jablanca and Vodenca). The track swings left to pass beneath a ski tow but continue directly ahead to pass a barn constructed of hayracks (topolar) and follow a path that leads into trees. Climb a small rise before descending to a surfaced road which is followed left to descend through the hamlet of Vodenca.

Beyond the last of the cottages take a small path leading left from the road (no waymarks) and descend through trees to cross an open field on a faint path heading for the Kovac Danilo campsite. Reach the campsite

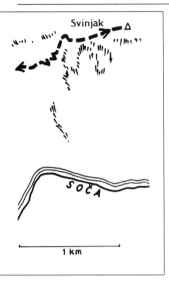

reception at the large house and turn right to descend over grass before arriving at a wire suspension bridge spanning the Koritnica River.

Cross this gingerly and turn right to follow a path above the river bank to a junction where a path leads left up a grassy crest. Continue by zig-zags through pine to reach a section of open grassland with the west ridge of Svinjak looming ahead. The path widens and is joined by a track on the right which leads to the village of Koritnica. Turn right at the main road and then immediately left to wind up between the flower decked chalets and barns and reach a water trough on the right in front of a grand old horse chestnut.

The route is now well waymarked with the characteristic Triglav targets. Follow a track leading behind the water trough to cross a small stream on the right by a stone wall and continue to ascend on the fringe of a pine forest to the left of a grassy slope. Pass a blockhouse (waymark) and continue into the next meadow alongside first a stone wall and then a fence, trending right to join a path that ascends to the right of a grassy slope littered with boulders. Climb steadily until tree cover obscures the view back to Bovec and the Soča Valley, where a meandering path continues under the welcome shade of beech and hawthorn. The path steepens to reach a dense forest section of pine to join the wide ridge crest at a junction where a detour left leads to a good viewpoint into the Koritnica and Bavisica Valleys.

Turn right and almost immediately fork left to continue the ascent by a series of long rising traverses and steep sections of zig-zags, to rejoin the ridge crest by a series of rock steps. Follow the crest through a beautiful grove of stunted beech on the lip of the Polog cliffs, with good views across to Rombon, Krnice and ahead to the summit of Bauski Grintavec.

The task of mounting the next rise in the ridge begins with a series of zig-zags broken by long traverses that lead over a more bouldery

169

*'Target' waymark below summit of Svinjak. Mt Rombon behind*

section, trending right to reach a magical wooded amphitheatre. The waymarking along the route is first class; the reassuring targets lead the walker confidently from tree to tree and tree to rock, appearing only as often as required to ensure the trail is not lost.

Leave the forest trending right and emerge onto open shrub covered ground with the prow of Svinjak rising to the left. The turquoise waters of the Soca River below appear to radiate a soft incandescence as it snakes a path through the lush green valley floor. The path now meanders over rock and shrub to re-enter the forest briefly before finally emerging beneath the broken slopes leading to the summit. Ascend a steep path on the ridge crest with stunning views into the Soča Valley, to cross a saddle before continuing over rock and tussocked grass. Frequent rest stops to take in the view on this steep section can be considered legitimate and wholly worthwhile. Climb a final series of zig-zags over shattered rock and across a grassy saddle to reach the summit of Svinjak and an unforgettable panorama.

The only disappointment is that there is no traverse of the summit and the route of ascent must be reversed to the village of Koritnica. Care should be exercised during the initial stages of the descent as the path is loose in parts and the effects of the moderate exposure is heightened.

Turn right by the water trough in Koritnica and ascend the surfaced track to reach a sharp right hand bend where a path leads left to descend by a hedgeline under the shade of alder. Continue through a slightly overgrown section to arrive at a surfaced road which is followed right to cross the Koritnica River. The road leads around to the right and reaches a junction at the site of an Austrian military cemetery and a memorial to Austrians killed in the area during the First World War.

Turn left (signposted Bovec) and follow the road to reach a track leading off right to Ravni Laz. After a short climb reach another junction where a left turn leads into open pasture. Pass through a triumphant arch of alder and continue alongside isolated barns, cottages and hayricks to arrive at the suburb of Mala Vas on the outskirts of Bovec. Follow around to the right before turning left to cross the channelled Geles stream and emerge at a main road beside the Felix Pub. Turn right and enter the pub by the main door or follow the road into the centre of Bovec.

## WALK 7: BOVEC - VISOKI KANIN (2,587m) - PRESTRELJENIK (2,499m) - BOVEC

| | |
|---|---|
| *Maps:* | Bovec z Okolico walking map (1:25,000), Julian Alps - West part (1:50,000), Triglav National Park (1:50,000) |
| *Walking Time:* | Visoki Kanin 3¹/₂ hours, Prestreljenik 1¹/₂ hours. |
| *Grading:* | Difficult. A general competence in mountain scrambling is required for these scenically rewarding walks. The route to Visoki Kanin is well waymarked although care is required in descent where many false trails and ledges tempt inattentive walkers. Difficult rock is protected with handrails and iron spikes and sections of the ridge are quite exposed. The route to Prestreljenik is technically easier than Visoki Kanin although not as well waymarked. Due to the exposed nature of the terrain either route could prove dangerous in a storm. |
| *Highest Altitude:* | Visoki Kanin 2,587m, Prestreljenik 2,499m. |
| *Lowest Altitude:* | 2,202m |
| *Approx. Distance:* | Visoki Kanin 7km, Prestreljenik 2km. |

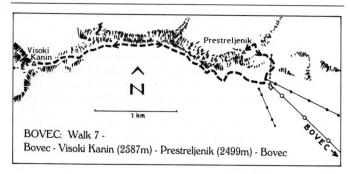

BOVEC: Walk 7 -
Bovec - Visoki Kanin (2587m) - Prestreljenik (2499m) - Bovec

The high peaks of the Kanin range dominate the northern fringe of the
Bovec basin and form the western frontier between Slovenia and Italy.
This parched limestone region is riddled with characteristic karst
features sculptured by the erosion of water feeding into the underground
drainage system. The route to Visoki Kanin traverses the upper screes
of the enormous Kaninski Podi basin to join the crest of the frontier ridge
before continuing in a sensational position to the summit. The peak is
noted as being one of the finest viewpoints in the Julian Alps.

Prestreljenik also stands on the frontier ridge and its proximity to
the Kanin gondola top station ensures its popularity. The path ascends
the east ridge to a summit viewpoint that is equally as extensive as its
more lofty neighbours.

Both walks make use of the Kanin gondola that rises in four sections
from Bovec to below the frontier ridge at 2,202m. The gondola runs
hourly between 0800 and 1600 (July/August) and every two hours at
weekends during June and September. The journey costs 84din single
or return and takes 30min to gain the 1,766m of vertical height to the top
station.

THE WALK
Reach the Kanin gondola bottom station by following the main road
west from the town centre in the direction of Tolmin to the small hamlet
of Dvor where a track ascends from the road to the right opposite a
petrol station.

**Visoki Kanin (2,587m)**
At the gondola top station follow a path leading west from a waymarked
boulder (Kanin 3 hr) and pass to the left of a chairlift to thread a course

around gaping rock crevasses, limestone slabs, boulders and loose scree. Pass a path descending to the Petraskalarja mountain hut on the left and continue on a rising traverse across scree above the barren rock amphitheatre of Prestreljeniski Podi. The Prestreljenik window, formed by weathering of the rock, can be seen in the cliffs above to the right. Local legend has it that God created the window to provide Noah with a secure mooring for the ark as the waters were receding after the great flood.

Reach a shattered buttress where the route traverses a ledge before climbing over rock (handrails) to continue more easily over large boulders that lead into the Kaninski Podi basin. Ignore an alternative route to the Petraskalarja Hut that descends to the left but continue to traverses on screes below the ridge that can be seen stretching to the summit of Visoki Kanin in the distance. Despite the barren nature of the habitat delicate gentian still manage to survive in tiny rock crevasses and their rich colour provides a welcome contrast in the landscape of sun bleached rock. Gradually the path begins to climb until a final series of short zig-zags lead to the ridge crest with views across the Kaninski glacier to the peaks and valleys of the western Julians.

Follow the ridge crest over easy angled slab to cross the summit of Kaninski Vrsic (2,543m) before descending steeply to a notch in the ridge. Cross this in an exposed position on the crest (handrail and iron spikes) and continue more easily over broken rock to cross a large slab. Descend to another notch beside a yawning cavern before leaving the ridge on the south side to reach a ledge that ascends to beneath an overhanging mosaic of rock. Regain the crest to reach the Kaninska Skrbina col (2,490m) where a path joins the ridge from the north side. Continue around left over a series of ledges that follow the ridge easily to the summit of Visoki Kanin. The view is truly unforgettable, extending to the Austrian mountains of Carinthia in the north, the peaks of the Dolomites in the west and south beyond the Friulian lowlands to the gulf of Trieste and the Adriatic sea. The central peaks of the Julian Alps dominate the eastern horizon.

Return to the gondola station by the route of ascent paying particular attention to waymarking. The path very often seems to follow the least obvious route and it is easy to be tempted along false trails.

## Prestreljenik (2,499m)

Prestreljenik rises above the gondola top station like the inverted hull of a huge boat, the layered rock strata rising in a series of uniform ledges

*Prestreljenik window*

to the summit. From the gondola top station ascend to a wide ski track on the far side of the chair lift to reach a saddle. Turn left to pass the top station and follow a path that leads onto the south-east slopes of Prestreljenik. Groups of tourists in sandals and shirtsleeves are left to their bewildered wanderings far below as the faint waymarks are followed to a ledge. Cross an easy slab below grassy terraces to an open saddle where the path begins to ascend in a series of short zig-zags. A terrace leads across a small gully, trending left over rock steps to reach a shingle path below a limestone cliff. Follow this over a grass covered section and ascend short rock steps to reach the cliff edge with views across the frontier into Italy. The path continues in zig-zags, over small outcrops, to cross a rocky gully before ascending a succession of easy rock steps below the ridge crest. Climb a short steep corner (iron spikes) to gain the ridge before veering left at an enormous boulder. Ascend broken rock that leads once more to the ridge which is then followed easily to the top, with extensive views in all directions.

Once again the route of ascent must be retraced to the gondola top station.

# LISTING OF CICERONE'S
# INTERNATIONAL GUIDES

## WALKING AND TREKKING IN THE ALPS
- WALKING IN THE ALPS
- 100 HUT WALKS IN THE ALPS
- CHAMONIX TO ZERMATT
- GRAND TOUR OF MONTE ROSA VOL. 1 AND VOL. 2
- TOUR OF MONT BLANC

## FRANCE, BELGIUM AND LUXEMBOURG
- WALKING IN THE ARDENNES
- ROCK CLIMBS BELGIUM & LUX.
- THE BRITTANY COASTAL PATH
- CHAMONIX - MONT BLANC WALKING GUIDE
- WALKING IN THE CEVENNES
- CORSICAN HIGH LEVEL ROUTE: GR20
- THE ECRINS NATIONAL PARK
- WALKING THE FRENCH ALPS: GR5
- WALKING THE FRENCH GORGES
- FRENCH ROCK
- WALKING IN THE HAUTE SAVOIE'
- WALKING IN THE LANGUEDOC
- TOUR OF THE OISANS: GR54
- WALKING IN PROVENCE
- THE PYRENEAN TRAIL: GR10
- THE TOUR OF THE QUEYRAS
- ROBERT LOUIS STEVENSON TRAIL
- WALKING IN TARENTAISE & BEAUFORTAIN ALPS
- ROCK CLIMBS IN THE VERDON
- TOUR OF THE VANOISE
- WALKS IN VOLCANO COUNTRY

## FRANCE/SPAIN
- ROCK CLIMBS IN THE PYRENEES
- WALKS & CLIMBS IN THE PYRENEES
- THE WAY OF ST JAMES LE PUY TO SANTIAGO - WALKER'S
- THE WAY OF ST JAMES LE PUY TO SANTIAGO - CYCLIST'S

## SPAIN AND PORTUGAL
- WALKING IN THE ALGARVE
- ANDALUSIAN ROCK CLIMBS
- BIRDWATCHING IN MALLORCA
- COSTA BLANCA ROCK
- COSTA BLANCA WALKS VOL 1
- COSTA BLANCA WALKS VOL 2
- WALKING IN MALLORCA
- ROCK CLIMBS IN MAJORCA, IBIZA & TENERIFE
- WALKING IN MADEIRA
- THE MOUNTAINS OF CENTRAL SPAIN
- THE SPANISH PYRENEES GR11 2ND EDITION
- WALKING IN THE SIERRA NEVADA
- WALKS & CLIMBS IN THE PICOS DE EUROPA
- VIA DE LA PLATA

## SWITZERLAND
- ALPINE PASS ROUTE, SWITZERLAND
- THE BERNESE ALPS A WALKING GUIDE
- CENTRAL SWITZERLAND
- THE JURA: HIGH ROUTE & SKI TRAVERSES
- WALKING IN TICINO, SWITZERLAND
- THE VALAIS, SWITZERLAND - A WALKING GUIDE

## GERMANY, AUSTRIA AND EASTERN EUROPE
- MOUNTAIN WALKING IN AUSTRIA
- WALKING IN THE BAVARIAN ALPS
- WALKING IN THE BLACK FOREST
- THE DANUBE CYCLE WAY
- GERMANY'S ROMANTIC ROAD
- WALKING IN THE HARZ MOUNTAINS
- KING LUDWIG WAY
- KLETTERSTEIG NORTHERN LIMESTONE ALPS
- WALKING THE RIVER RHINE TRAIL
- THE MOUNTAINS OF ROMANIA
- WALKING IN THE SALZKAMMERGUT
- HUT-TO-HUT IN THE STUBAI ALPS
- THE HIGH TATRAS

## SCANDANAVIA
- WALKING IN NORWAY
- ST OLAV'S WAY

## ITALY AND SLOVENIA
- ALTA VIA - HIGH LEVEL WALKS DOLOMITES
- CENTRAL APENNINES OF ITALY
- WALKING CENTRAL ITALIAN ALPS
- WALKING IN THE DOLOMITES
- SHORTER WALKS IN THE DOLOMITES
- WALKING ITALY'S GRAN PARADISO
- LONG DISTANCE WALKS IN ITALY'S GRAN PARADISO
- ITALIAN ROCK
- WALKS IN THE JULIAN ALPS
- WALKING IN SICILY
- WALKING IN TUSCANY
- VIA FERRATA SCRAMBLES IN THE DOLOMITES

## OTHER MEDITERRANEAN COUNTRIES
- THE ATLAS MOUNTAINS
- WALKING IN CYPRUS
- CRETE - THE WHITE MOUNTAINS
- THE MOUNTAINS OF GREECE
- JORDAN - WALKS, TREKS, CAVES ETC.
- THE MOUNTAINS OF TURKEY
- TREKS & CLIMBS WADI RUM JORDAN
- CLIMBS & TREKS IN THE ALA DAG
- WALKING IN PALESTINE

## HIMALAYA
- ADVENTURE TREKS IN NEPAL

- ANNAPURNA - A TREKKER'S GUIDE
- EVEREST - A TREKKERS' GUIDE
- GARHWAL & KUMAON - A TREKKER'S GUIDE
- KANGCHENJUNGA - A TREKKER'S GUIDE
- LANGTANG, GOSAINKUND & HELAMBU TREKKERS GUIDE
- MANASLU - A TREKKER'S GUIDE

## OTHER COUNTRIES
- MOUNTAIN WALKING IN AFRICA - KENYA
- OZ ROCK – AUSTRALIAN CRAGS
- WALKING IN BRITISH COLUMBIA
- TREKKING IN THE CAUCAUSUS
- GRAND CANYON & AMERICAN SOUTH WEST
- ROCK CLIMBS IN HONG KONG
- ADVENTURE TREKS WEST NORTH AMERICA
- CLASSIC TRAMPS IN NEW ZEALAND

## TECHNIQUES AND EDUCATION
- SNOW & ICE TECHNIQUES
- ROPE TECHNIQUES
- THE BOOK OF THE BIVVY
- THE HILLWALKER'S MANUAL
- THE TREKKER'S HANDBOOK
- THE ADVENTURE ALTERNATIVE
- BEYOND ADVENTURE
- FAR HORIZONS - ADVENTURE TRAVEL FOR ALL
- MOUNTAIN WEATHER

Cicerone's mission is to inform and inspire by providing the best guides to exploring the world

Since its foundation over 30 years ago, Cicerone has specialised in publishing guidebooks and has built a reputation for quality and reliability. It now publishes nearly 300 guides to the major destinations for outdoor enthusiasts, including Europe, UK and the rest of the world.

Written by leading and committed specialists, Cicerone guides are recognised as the most authoritative. They are full of information, maps and illustrations so that the user can plan and complete a successful and safe trip or expedition – be it a long face climb, a walk over Lakeland fells, an alpine traverse, a Himalayan trek or a ramble in the countryside.

With a thorough introduction to assist planning, clear diagrams, maps and colour photographs to illustrate the terrain and route, and accurate and detailed text, Cicerone guides are designed for ease of use and access to the information.

If the facts on the ground change, or there is any aspect of a guide that you think we can improve, we are always delighted to hear from you.

**Cicerone Press**
2 Police Square  Milnthorpe  Cumbria  LA7 7PY
Tel:01539 562 069   Fax:01539 563 417
e-mail:info@cicerone.co.uk   web:www.cicerone.co.uk

CICERONE